Church Bible Study Handbook

Robin Maas

ABINGDON PRESS
Nashville

Church Bible Study Handbook

Library of Congress Cataloging in Publication Data

MAAS, ROBIN, 1939-
  Church Bible study handbook.

  Bibliography: p.
  1. Bible—Study. I. Title.
  BS600.2.M23 1982   220′.07   82-6860   AACR2

ISBN 0-687-08146-7

MANUFACTURED BY THE PARTHENON PRESS AT
NASHVILLE, TENNESSEE, UNITED STATES OF AMERICA

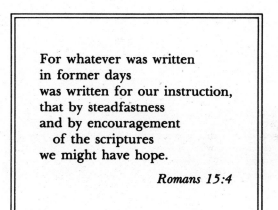

For whatever was written
in former days
was written for our instruction,
that by steadfastness
and by encouragement
  of the scriptures
we might have hope.

Romans 15:4

ACKNOWLEDGMENTS

This book owes its existence largely to the persistence and enthusiasm of a group of dedicated United Methodist laypersons who served (from 1979 to 1981) on the planning committee of the Baltimore Conference's Annual Laity Retreat and to the retreat's sponsoring organization, the Division of Laity. In particular, my friend and co-worker Nancy L. Iden worked tirelessly to support the training of lay Bible study leaders and teachers for the Baltimore Conference and the production of a handbook to facilitate this form of training. I will always be grateful to Nancy for her commitment to the empowerment of the laity.

Several other individuals deserve thanks for their assistance: Dr. Lawrence H. Stookey, professor of preaching and worship at Wesley Theological Seminary, has been my chief adviser on matters pertaining to the ecumenical lectionary; also of Wesley, Dr. Dewey M. Beegle critiqued my material on the English versions of the Bible. I am grateful to my former student Ruth Dixon and my daughter, Julianna, for their assistance in preparing materials used in chapters 5 and 6 respectively and to Mort Leggett, an active layman in the United Church of Christ, who read the manuscript and offered editorial suggestions.

Two local congregations deserve special mention since they helped sharpen my understanding of the role of scripture in the life of the church and the kinds of issues that arise in congregational Bible study. My thanks to the Council on Ministries of Faith United Methodist Church in Rockville, Maryland, for patiently submitting to some exploratory efforts in my quest to develop a more integrated approach to the study of scripture. My own congregation, Dumbarton United Methodist Church in Washington, D.C., has taught me much about what it means to be in active dialogue with scripture. In particular, Dumbarton's dedicated Sunday school teachers provided support by being my first audience—and my sharpest critics.

Finally, I owe a special debt of gratitude to my former teacher and mentor, Bruce C. Birch. Professor of Old Testament at Wesley Seminary, Dr. Birch was my first instructor in Bible. His vision of the role of scripture in the life of the church has been catalytic in the development of my work, and his encouragement and support were available to me from the first page to the last.

CONTENTS

This book was written for my students: lay men and women who love the Bible and are eager to share what they have learned with others.

It is dedicated to the memory of two lifelong learners whose devotion to scripture has made it all the more precious to me:

my mother, Dorothy Lloyd Hill

and

my student Oliver Scott Miles

The Origin of the Lay Exegesis Project:
A Personal Account

I was still a student in seminary when I was asked to lead my first Bible study class. A student-pastor friend in a nearby suburban church was looking for something stimulating for a small group of housewives who wanted to know more about the scriptures. A laywoman, I had attended seminary because of a similar desire to become more expert in matters biblical, and I had for some time assumed that I would eventually teach scripture in some capacity. My vision of a teaching ministry was still rather hazy at the point I received the invitation to serve this particular group, but it was nothing if not conventional. I pictured myself lecturing in front of a chalkboard, unfolding a panoramic view of Israel's encounters with God to avid literary types and history buffs. I didn't know very much about the church.

So when the opportunity to teach came, I decided we would "do" the Gospel of John. I selected a lively, very well written supplemental book (designed by a noted New Testament scholar for lay study) and, all innocent, prepared a thorough introductory lesson on the Fourth Gospel.

Do not imagine that these housewives shattered all my preconceptions about what it meant to teach scripture. It is true that they all complained that the book I had chosen was "too hard." It is also true that a couple of them dropped out because the study really was *study*, and what they had had in mind was actually group devotions. But the majority of them stuck it out bravely to the end and seemed genuinely sorry to see me go when the last session finally rolled around. In ten weeks we had worked our way slowly and methodically

11

through several chapters of John, and although the women had certainly learned something, I felt I had learned considerably more.

The most important thing I learned—something that was not addressed in any of my seminary courses—was that when I said good-bye, their Bible study would come to a halt and they would be forced to cool their heels until the pastor or some other suitably qualified authority figure was available to lead another study. These women, most of whom did not have more than a high-school education, now seemed utterly bereft. Throughout the series of lessons I had felt disturbed by their lack of self-confidence and touching faith in my "scholarly" interpretations. What, I wondered, had I *really* accomplished by breezing in there, dispensing wisdom, and then leaving? Besides giving them some interesting information, I had most likely reinforced their own feelings of inadequacy: "She knows so much! We know so little!" This experience, more than anything else I can remember, set me to rethinking what Bible study was all about and put me on a path from which there has been no turning back.

My first conventional Bible study turned out to be my last, for I immediately set to work designing a totally different type of Bible study experience—a course that would have as its goal the teaching of whatever skills were necessary to give laypersons the self-confidence and drive to conduct their own, ongoing Bible study programs without constant recourse to professional assistance. I analyzed the skills I had acquired through my own efforts and in seminary; I identified the reference tools that I felt were absolutely essential to the study process; and then I began to work out a systematic, sequential method of presenting (and reinforcing) those skills. In addition I assessed the various attitudes laypeople exhibit toward Bible study and looked for ways to foster those which would facilitate the development of challenging, theologically inclusive, lay-led Bible study programs. My ambition was to work with a group of lay Bible students and then leave them *still working*—to set something in motion that would continue to develop and bear fruit long after I had gone. In short, I decided that what really needed to be taught were the fundamentals of what is known in professional circles as *biblical exegesis*, i.e., a disciplined method of studying and explicating biblical texts.

In retrospect I feel fortunate that I was relatively ignorant of entrenched and limiting views within the church about what it is possible to do with or for the laity. Although I was aware that many laypersons might not be *interested* in Bible study, it never occurred to me that they would not be *capable* of serious study once motivated. I reasoned that what I had learned, they could learn—and I was equally convinced that it should not be necessary to enroll in seminary in order to learn it! *Full access to scripture could—and should—come through membership in a local congregation.*

It was not very long before another teaching opportunity presented itself. This time I went off to the first session armed with a full set of reference books: a concordance, a Bible dictionary, a Bible atlas, and a one-volume commentary; and the contrast between the second teaching experience and the first one was dramatic. Although my first efforts at teaching an exegetical methodology seem relatively crude in light of what I do now, I did manage to get that set of reference books into everyone's hands at least once during the course of several weeks and had the satisfaction of watching people learn how to use them. By the end of the course, many members of the class had purchased copies of these reference tools for themselves and as gifts for friends and relatives, for in addition to some much too long and over-researched presentations, much excitement and enthusiasm had been generated. Much to my surprise, I was informed by my students that what I was doing seemed "revolutionary." I had naïvely assumed, first of all, that all ministers knew how to do biblical exegesis; and second, I had even more naïvely assumed that ministers probably spend a great deal of their time instructing their parishioners in the skills they (presumably) had acquired. This was the real beginning of my own education in the realities of what passes for Bible study in many churches. What did I learn?

I learned that the prospect of engaging the "naked" biblical text (without the assistance of study book or commentary) is, for most laypersons—and many clergy too—relatively threatening simply because they don't have the first idea of how to go about it! The common assumption among the laity is that nothing less than a seminary education will serve as adequate preparation for this kind of encounter. Ironically, the average seminarian probably spends less time on specifically "biblical" studies than is generally imagined, for the harsh reality of the situation is simply this: neither the institutional church nor the local congregation has made the study of scripture one of its highest priorities, and as long as Bible study continues to be seen as just one of several (competing) activities undertaken by the church, rather than as the foundational work *that undergirds everything else the church tries to do,* this will continue to be the case. I further learned that any real change in this situation must be the result of pressure "from below." Happily, there are many signs that such pressure is beginning to build.

Signs of the Times: Exegesis Is for Everyone

As it usually does, one thing led to another. My initial efforts at developing an exegetical approach to Bible study generated a surprising amount of interest. In the fall of 1978 I was approached by the Division of Laity of the Baltimore Annual Conference of The United Methodist Church and asked to develop a training program for lay Bible study leaders. Their intention was to develop as quickly as possible a cadre of skilled laypersons to serve at their Laity Retreat—a large-scale, basically grass-roots event held annually for the purpose of empowering the laity to minister effectively in a variety of capacities.

The development of this lay training program made obvious the need for a handbook on exegetical method suited to the needs of laypersons and local congregations. The demand for training courses of this nature soon exceeded my capacity to respond, and it became necessary to develop and offer an *advanced* training course so that lay Bible students who were particularly motivated and committed to an exegetical approach could begin serving as teachers of the basic lay training course.

Over the past three years, approximately three hundred laypersons in the Baltimore Annual Conference have received instruction in the fundamentals of biblical exegesis, and several hundred more have at least been "exposed" to this approach through participation in Bible study at the Annual Laity Retreat. Although the educational level and theological backgrounds of the lay Bible study leaders in this program have varied widely, their enthusiasm and commitment has been uniformly high and has thus provided the primary motive force behind the writing of this book. These are the people who have taught me about the real needs of local congregations and the special problems laypersons face as they attempt to make the study of scripture central to their witness and worship. They are the ones who have done the arduous work of *testing* the materials presented here. They are the ones who are *validating* the methodology by demonstrating that the motivation and capabilities are really there once the way is opened by the acquisition of new skills.

As the Lay Bible Study Project has continued to develop, it has become increasingly obvious that "Bible study" always needs to be rooted firmly in the total context of congregational life. Too often the subject has been dealt with in the abstract or as a totally private enterprise. While it is true that exegetical study methods can be taught in isolation, it is also true that exegesis can remain a relatively sterile intellectual exercise if its results are not brought to bear on the full range of activities undertaken by the living—and local—body of Christ. This handbook tries to outline an approach to Bible study that takes the congregational context into account (chapters 2 and 3). We are interested in presenting more than a study method *per se,* though that remains our primary concern (chapters 4–7). We are also concerned that congregations become aware of and sensitive to basic attitudes about scripture that play a vital role not only in the way scripture is studied (chapter 1), but also in the way we deal with evident differences in theological perspectives among equally earnest folk (chapter 9). Finally, we are concerned to know what impact if any a particular set of attitudes and an exegetical approach to the study of scripture may have on the one thing that justifies the church's existence—the possibility of conversion and genuine change (chapter 8).

CHAPTER ONE

Beyond the Devotional Bible Study:

The Local Congregation Is Called to Do Its Own Theologizing

"Ye have heard that it was said by them of old time . . . But *I* say unto you . . ." (Matt. 5:21-22 KJV; emphasis added)

From the time a mysterious stranger, "beginning with Moses and all the prophets," interpreted portions of the Old Testament to two of the Nazarene's followers (Luke 24:27), the study and exposition of Scripture has been the essential foundation of the church's reflection on the nature of its identity and mission. A primary symbol of the Christian faith, the Bible is held in high regard by virtually every denomination; consequently, we might expect it to function as a *unifying* force among believers. Quite the opposite is the case: The Bible—God's word of judgment and hope to all humankind—is called upon to justify and condemn radically different views of the faith. In addition, and more to the point, the Bible is used to defend differing perceptions of its own role within the faith community. In theory, these various perceptions of the place of scripture in the life of the church all treat this sacred document with respect. In practice, we find a wide range of opinion about the importance of scripture—everything from "the Bible says . . ." to "*Who cares* what the Bible says"!

At the very least, it must be conceded that the Bible takes

17

itself very seriously and that the church as a whole does too. Problems arise when we try to define what "taking the Bible seriously" actually means. Does it mean taking it literally? Or does it mean spending more time studying it? Is the church's devotion to scripture to be measured by the claims we make for it? Or would a better measure be the general level of what is commonly referred to as "biblical literacy"? Further, should the church assume that spending time on the study of scripture will ensure that its vision and witness will be authentically "biblical"?

The lack of consensus about the role of scripture in the life of the church has resulted in a deplorable confusion—and profusion—of method in the matter of Bible study. The very words "Bible study" evoke a variety of responses from church people, some of them quite negative; for although many people feel the need to know the Bible better, the prospect of systematic Bible study is more than a little daunting. Why should this be the case? In order to answer this question, it is first necessary to address another question, that of how our understanding of the role of scripture in the life of the church directly affects the way in which the study of it is approached.

The list of models shown below is not intended to be exhaustive, but it is generally representative of the ways in which the church has typically understood the role of the Bible in the faith community. Presented in schematic fashion, these models are necessarily oversimplified and will seldom be found in the "pure" forms suggested here. Rather, they tend to exist in combination with one another. For example, the view of scripture described in model no. 1 is quite compatible with that of no. 3, as is no. 2 with no. 4.

The Role of Scripture in the Local Congregation

A Typology of Popular Perspectives

I. *The Bible functions primarily as a rule book or infallible guide to Christian living.* As the Word of God, the Bible informs Christians in a precise and straightforward way of God's will for them as individuals and as the church.

18

Implications for study: Bible study tends to be highly content-oriented, nonanalytical, literalistic, and moralistic. The church must know precisely "what the Bible says" in order to obey God's rules for Christian living.

II. *The Bible functions primarily as a source of religious principles and ideals.* The value of scripture lies in its embodiment of lofty religious ideals and ethical principles—principles by which Christians must judge their actions and order their lives.

Implications for study: Bible study tends to be "thematic" or topical in emphasis. The focus is on abstracting general ideas from historically specific material. Study is usually undertaken for very pragmatic purposes, e.g., to lend support for a position already espoused or a program already undertaken.

III. *The Bible functions primarily as the source of "completed revelation."* Scripture is a compendium of supernatural or divine truths that the church articulates and interprets authoritatively in the form of "Christian doctrine."

Implications for study: Attention to specific texts is usually for purposes of proof-texting or justifying specific doctrinal formulations. Since scripture authenticates doctrine, to know the doctrine is, in essence, to know the "content" of the Bible.

IV. *The Bible functions primarily as a resource for individual or small-group devotions.* The Bible is a collection of stories, prayers, hymns, and teaching and preaching material which is meant to confront, console, and inspire the individual Christian with "mountaintop" experiences.

Implications for study: Bible study is really a misnomer here. The emphasis is on identifying and utilizing inspirational biblical material for prayer, reflection, and witnessing. Priority is giving to the text's "spiritual" meaning at the expense of its more human and historical dimensions. The relationship that

19

develops between Bible and reader is a highly personal and privatized one.

V. *The Bible functions primarily as a venerated symbol of past and present identity.* The Bible (usually in a lavishly illustrated and expensive format) reclines in a place of honor on the communal altar or family bookshelf. Like patriotism and motherhood, its authority is invoked sporadically to lend validity and credibility to the church's pre-established stance on issues relating to mission or morals.

Implications for study: None. Bible study is seldom an option, let alone a priority in such situations. The truly curious or devout are driven to join "underground" Bible study groups, which are usually very privatized and pietistic.

Some Troubling Consequences

The models presented above all share some significant limitations. *First,* and most important, they all treat scripture as a *static* entity. Like any written document, the Bible has objective permanence; and because scripture carries with it the weight of special authority there is a constant tendency to deal with it in a purely formal or "legal" sense—as if the entire thing (and not just the Ten Commandments) had been engraved in stone. When the church focuses exclusively on the Bible's "writtenness," its contents are usually uncritically absolutized.

Second, these models deal with scripture in a relatively selective way. Whether the focus is on revelation or rules, these models operate to reinforce, rather than challenge, existing theological agendas. Of course it is true that the Bible contains rules for Christian living as well as profound ethical ideals and principles. Portions of scripture can (and should) be used for devotional purposes, and very few Christians would be prepared to argue that the Bible does not give authoritative witness to God's revelation of himself in creation and Christ, in the history of the people Israel and the church. But the message of scripture is distorted when we assume that *one* of these dimensions accurately characterizes the whole. Like the blind men and the elephant, the church has "battled" for the

Bible with a very partial and limited view of the scope and complexity of the reality.

Third, because these models are relatively selective, they are also *a*historical. The tendency to deal with selected texts in isolation from their literary and historical contexts has contributed to a static view of both scripture and inspiration. The failure to utilize these contexts as aids in interpreting biblical material has, in the long run, left the church bereft of the Bible's greatest source of inspiration and insight—*the conviction that God spoke a particular word to a peculiar people* and that it was the very word they needed to hear at the precise time they needed to hear it! Unfortunately (and ironically), the attempt to dehistoricize scripture so that it may seem eternally true has made it that much harder for the church to comprehend that what God did for Israel, i.e., speak *directly* to her condition, God can do for the church today.

Taken together, these flawed and partial views of the role of scripture have done considerable damage to the enterprise of Bible study in the local congregation. The most visible consequences may be either complacency and self-satisfaction or discouragement, frustration, and boredom, and these in turn produce a still more vexing problem for the church that wishes to honor God's word in its corporate life. I speak here of the problem of guilt.

The individual Christian and the church as a whole are beginning to feel an enormous burden of guilt: first, because we can no longer disguise the fact that only a tiny fraction of our number can count themselves biblically literate; and second, because despite the plethora of new materials on the subject, we have not yet succeeded in finding a workable model for *systematic* Bible study in the local congregation. Most of what we have tried we don't like—or if we liked it well enough, we nevertheless lacked the incentive to continue either on our own or with the aid of a group. What really frightens us is the prospect that it may be the Bible itself we don't like, and should that prove to be the case, the results could be catastrophic! For centuries the church has held up to its members the ideal of a community thoroughly grounded in ancient scriptural traditions, living out the biblical vision of wholeness and salvation. We sense (even if dimly) that our identity as Christians is

21

rooted in scripture—that not to know the Bible is not to understand who we are. On the other hand, the prospect of knowing it but not liking it seems riskier still. The sporadic Lenten or Advent Bible study is one way of quieting these fears.

The Search for a Viable Alternative

The Bible in Active Dialogue with the Church

The earliest Christians were faced with a profound dilemma in relation to their scriptures—what we now refer to as the Old Testament. Their preconceptions about God's plan of salvation, shaped and nurtured by the traditions of their ancestors, had been shattered by the reality of their experiences with a crucified and risen messiah. The impact of their direct experiences with Jesus of Nazareth and the risen Christ had so completely transformed their lives and outlooks that one is justified in assuming that they might have felt free to dispense with the sometimes embarrassing visions and restrictive traditions of the Old Testament as something that would keep them tied to a past and partial "revelation." Nothing could have been farther from the truth.

The entire New Testament witnesses to the devotion of the early church to its scriptures. The writers of the Gospels and Epistles make frequent reference (either by direct quotation or allusion) to a wide range of scripture in their effort *to explain* what God was doing in Christ. An analysis of their choice of references and the manner in which they used them show, not surprisingly, a definite preference for certain portions of the Old Testament (especially the Psalms and Isaiah), but overall one cannot escape the conclusion that the church was engaged in an intense struggle to *maintain* its ties to the past in order to preserve its traditional identity as God's chosen people or the children of Abraham and to ensure (at all costs) the authority and viability of the Old Testament for the new faith community.

We also discover from reading the New Testament that some Old Testament perspectives and practices did indeed have to be dispensed with, e.g., dietary restrictions and the

22

requirement of circumcision for converts (see Acts 10, 11, and 15). Such decisions represent a clear break with the past and a rejection of a scriptural "mandate." Paul's Letters and the book of Acts reveal that such requirements for change were not always simultaneously crystal clear to every confessing Christian, that there were factions in the early faith community, and that vital, Spirit-directed change was often a slow and painful process. What is significant in the witness of the New Testament is the *dialogue* or "conversation" we see occurring between new Christians and their ancient faith traditions. At various points in the history of the church, individuals or groups have tried to dispense with the Old Testament altogether.[1] The first Christians knew better. Just as Paul knew he had to take account of the views of Cephas, James, and the other "pillars" in Jerusalem, so the fledgling church discovered that it had to come to terms with its past so that what they now were and would someday become could truly be a fulfillment of what they once had been.

The church's dialogue with its faith traditions (i.e., with scripture) is characterized by struggle and inventiveness. Consider the creativity—and cleverness—of Paul as he applies himself to the task of justifying scripturally the acceptance of uncircumcised Gentiles into the messianic community (see Galatians 3–4; Romans 4). Faced with an apparently clear conflict between scripture and tradition on the one hand and a compelling call to mission on the other, what does he do?

Holding the tradition (Genesis 12, 15, 17) up to the light, he first examines it with the utmost care. (Remember, Paul was trained by a rabbi!) But that examination was far more than a simple academic exercise: Paul *examines* the tradition by loving and admiring it, talking to it, wrestling with it. Paul's knowledge of scripture and his conviction of conscience gave him the freedom to place the tradition in a new context so that it could be recast and reinterpreted in an astonishingly daring way. There are two things to applaud here: First, Paul's thorough *knowledge* of scripture and the skill that allows him to handle it so adroitly; and second, his continued *loyalty* to it, even when the needs of the moment require some kind of drastic modification or reinterpretation. In order to do what he did, Paul had to "know his Bible," and it is no exaggeration to say that the future of Christianity as a world religion in some sense hinged on just such creative "connecting" activity.

It should be noted that this kind of active dialogue or conversation between the demands of the past and the realities of the present—between tradition and experience—was not the invention of the early church. It was, in fact, an important part of their faith inheritance, *for precisely the same dynamic occurs in the Old Testament itself,* which is, among other things, a vast collection of reinterpreted traditions addressed to changing circumstances. The most notable instance of this is the way in which the Old Testament constantly holds up for reexamination the experience of deliverance at the Red Sea and the formation of the covenant community on Mount Sinai. This foundational experience is the ultimate measure of authenticity for Israel, the "rock" out of which endless springs of inspiration are made to flow in an otherwise dry and thirsty expanse of political oppression. Consider, for example, the re-creation of the Exodus theme in that portion of the book of Isaiah (chapters 40–55) which was addressed to exiles in Babylon:

> Thus says the Lord,
>   who makes a way in the sea,
>   a path in the mighty waters,
> who brings forth chariot and horse,
>   army and warrior;
> they lie down, they cannot rise,
>   they are extinguished, quenched
>   like a wick:
>
> "Remember not the former things,
>   nor consider the things of old.
> Behold, I am doing a new thing;
>   now it springs forth, do you not
>   perceive it?
> I will make a way in the wilderness
>   and rivers in the desert.
> The wild beasts will honor me,
>   the jackals and the ostriches;
> for I give water in the wilderness,
>   rivers in the desert,
> to give drink to my chosen people,

> the people whom I formed for myself
> that they might declare my praise." (43:16-21)

> "Is my hand shortened, that it
>   cannot redeem?
> Or have I no power to deliver?
> Behold, by my rebuke I dry up the
>   sea,
> I make the rivers a desert . . ." (50:2)

Here again, a precious tradition is held up to the light, examined, and deftly re-presented in a different setting so that it might bring new vision and fresh hope to a people filled with blindness and despair.

Similar examples could be cited of the way in which creation themes, the promise to Abraham, or traditions about the Davidic kingship are re-presented in Scripture for the renewal of the faith community. The point is this: *The Bible itself (Old and New Testaments alike) provides the church with a workable alternative to the static models it has tended to rely on as a basis for the study of scripture.* This biblical model is dynamic and change-oriented, but at the same time it accords the highest respect and importance to sacred traditions. Scripture teaches us to respect scripture, first of all, *by knowing it thoroughly;* second, *by engaging it directly as a means of interpreting our immediate experience.*

Why, we might ask, has the church been willing to settle for static models instead? Probably because the biblical change-model (if and when it is recognized as such) requires more skill, more patience, more imagination, and more trust in the future than most of us believe we can command. It requires the church to *do* theology in much the same way Paul did: that is, constantly to reexamine our faith traditions *in light of what is happening to us now* and then to make bold statements about what those traditions (or texts) *mean now.* Even more forbidding is the prospect of having to live out that meaning in the context of worship, witness, and mission!

This book presupposes a more optimistic view of the local congregation's potential as "producers" (and not just consumers) of biblical theology.[2] It presents methods of studying scripture that flow from this model of active dialogue and exchange between the traditions of the faith community and its immediate experience; and, further, it assumes that the skills needed for active dialogue with scripture can—and must—be taught to and exercised by the whole church, not just the clergy. Finally, it assumes that the patience needed to deal with biblical texts in a sustained and disciplined manner can be acquired, through practice, providing the community is willing to support and encourage such study. Granted, the kind of creative imagination required for making artful and apt connections and applications of the biblical material is not an "achievement" but a gift of the Spirit, but since the Spirit is known to be a cheerful giver, even the local church can aspire to the task of theologizing!

Implications for Study

Just as the previous models cited tended to produce specific and predictable approaches to the study of scripture, so it is with this model. Following are a few of the implications for study of which a congregation must be aware when it undertakes to engage in active dialogue with the Bible:

1. In the conversation between the confessing community and its faith traditions, *The Bible has the first word.* The local congregation needs to structure study opportunities and employ methodologies that *allow biblical texts to speak clearly and forcefully for themselves.* Since the meaning of texts is not always (in fact relatively seldom) self-evident, allowing the Bible to have the first word is not always as easy as it sounds. What is required is a disciplined method that has, as its goal, a more or less thorough examination of the terms of the text: its vocabulary, grammatical structure, literary form, historical context, and theological concerns. This type of disciplined study is not new; it has been practiced in one form or another by theologians and biblical commentators for centuries under the name of biblical *exegesis,* a Greek term used to describe a process of expository interpretation (*ex*—"out" + *hēgeîsthai*— "guide"). What *is* new is the idea that laypersons can be equipped by and in the local congregation to follow what—at first blush—sounds like such an academic study process. Yet the kind of respect for tradition that we see exhibited in

26

scripture itself requires just such an investment of time and careful effort. *The worst fallacy the church has perpetrated in respect to biblical education is the notion that the laity can learn to understand the Bible only by reading books about the Bible instead of wrestling with actual biblical texts themselves.*

2. In the conversation between the confessing community and its faith traditions, *the entire community actively "listens."* "Listening" in this sense is not to be equated with the passive stance of the person in the pew who settles back on Sunday morning to hear what the preacher is going to make of *that* reading! Listening, in the dialogue between the church and its scriptures, means personal involvement in the uncovering of new information and the analysis of its significance for the interpretation of texts. For too long the laity have willingly abdicated their responsibility for taking active part in the dialogue with scripture. We have been content to let the pastor do our listening for us and quick to complain when the results of this private conversation (evidenced in preaching and teaching) have been less comforting or compelling than we wish. Generally speaking, it has not occurred to the laity that our own contribution to the mission of the local congregation (whether through its program or administrative structure) might be substantially enhanced and strengthened—or even radically altered—as a result of our direct involvement in the dialogue/study process. Generally speaking, it has not occurred to the laity that the weekly worship service, including the sermon, could be a truly *communal* response to God's word rather than an expression of the piety and skill of a single person—the preacher.

3. In the conversation between the confessing community and its faith traditions, *the community responds.* Scripture demonstrates that God's chosen people exercised considerable freedom in their dialogue with the authoritative Word. They cited it, praised and extolled it, and relied on and took refuge in it as in "the shadow of a great rock in a weary land" (Isa. 32:2 KJV). But they also challenged it, railed against it, and sometimes even rejected it, for *the realities of the present were for both Israel and the early church a constant and very important factor in the dialogue with foundational traditions.* At times there were, and will certainly continue to be, clear tensions between what the

27

faith community feels called to do and what the tradition (scripture) asserts or claims is necessary. There is no dodging this, but the biblical model allows *at least equal status* for the claims of immediate experience in the conversation with scripture. Once the church has honored scripture by a thorough exegetical examination of its contents, i.e., has actively "listened" to what the biblical witness is saying, then *the community has the further responsibility of responding as a full partner in the dialogue.* Depending on particular circumstances, the response of the church may take the form of praise or complaint, of willing or sorrowful compliance, wholehearted acceptance, or, more rarely but sometimes inevitably, outright rejection.

4. In the conversation between the confessing community and its faith traditions, the *Spirit has the last word.* The Bible, as the most authoritative statement of the faith community's origins, makes strong and unmistakable claims on the community's loyalty, time, and resources. It has always been and must always continue to be a major factor in the life and witness of individual Christian congregations, and any church that proceeds to initiate and pursue a life of faith without reference to its contents and claims is without excuse. The community that honors scripture *by letting it have the first word and thus speak directly to them* will find it a constant source of challenge, refreshment, and renewal.

At the same time, the church has a responsibility to fulfill in engaging the entire community in the dialogue with scripture. Scripture *compels* a collective—and not just a personal—response. The basis for that response is the stuff of experience—what is actually happening in the church and the world today. We do not honor scripture by consulting it out of mere curiosity. Like Peter and Paul, we look back on our tradition out of a specific, historical context—a setting in which a myriad of pressing problems vie for the church's attention and resources. When the biblical text speaks, the whole church needs to hear that Word as a particular word addressed to our own "peculiar" circumstances—to the precise place where we have been placed and called to minister. Therefore, while it is essential that the church reflect on its particular experiences in the light of its faith traditions, it is equally necessary for the church *to reevaluate and reinterpret the tradition in light of the demands of the present.* The dynamics of this dialogue provide the proper context for action and mission. If we know *what* scripture is saying, we can act in good faith, even when we feel that the realities of immediate experience require a break with the past.

The fact that earnest Christians may differ in their understanding of what either scripture or the needs of the present require may give us pause, but it should not be seen as an excuse for discouragement or a cause for despair. As we have seen, the required break with tradition over the issue of circumcision was not universally acknowledged to be necessary. People acted in good faith on both sides of the issue, and although Paul was certainly "vindicated" by history, he did not go it alone but continued to refer all that he did to the authorities in Jerusalem.

More recent history reveals that very divisive issues result in the same process of appeal to tradition. The issue of slavery split denominations, with both sides citing scripture for support. The ordination of women and the status of homosexuals in the church are problems that will not be satisfactorily settled soon and certainly not until the biblical traditions have been taken into full account. Nevertheless, if there is one thing to which scripture can be confidently said to attest, it is that the Spirit moves with creativity and freedom through the medium of the church, and that *when change must come* (whether in the form of a break with tradition or a dramatic renewal of it) *it will come,* for the spirit always has the last word.

Conclusions

Although it is true that our view of the role of scripture in the life of the church directly influences the way in which we study it, it is also true that the method of study we employ will, over time, shape and reshape our initial perspectives. It is possible, and sometimes very desirable, to introduce and use a methodology without making explicit all of its theoretical underpinnings.

The exegetical methodologies set forth in this book can

certainly be introduced and taught to groups without elaborate theoretical explanations. In fact, in most cases, it is probably best to begin with practical experiences and let the model "reveal itself." Like the church's sacraments, the appropriate role of scripture in the community of faith is probably best understood and appreciated *after* it has been directly experienced. Practice in exegetical study will almost inevitably change perspectives on Scripture. Sometimes it will change lives.

One final caveat: For the sake of clarity, the dialogue model outlined in this chapter has been presented in linear fashion—first *this,* then *that.* . . . It needs to be emphasized that this dialogue or conversation is probably best described as "circular." Consequently, a community may enter this conversation at various points. To insist that study must always precede change or specific action is to encourage a community to *only study and never act,* for how many of us are willing to claim a *definitive* knowledge of scripture at any point in our lives? Action and change may (and often do) precede study, but study is just as helpful in interpreting change as it is in initiating it.

CHAPTER TWO

Equipped to Converse:
Making Biblical Resources Available to the Laity

So Philip ran to him, and heard him reading Isaiah the prophet, and asked, "Do you understand what you are reading?" . . . "How can I, unless some one guides me?" (Acts 8:30*b*-31*a*)

Acongregation wishing to engage in active dialogue with its biblical traditions must first concern itself with the problem of resources. Its goal should be to make scripture available to the laity in the *fullest* sense of the word. To be sure, this is no new concern; the church has been laboring for centuries to fulfill this obligation, although with mixed results.

For example, the Protestant reformers threw themselves wholeheartedly into the task of bringing the Bible to the *laos,* the whole "people of God." Luther's translation of the Bible from the original Greek and Hebrew texts into the German vernacular, and the invention of movable type, taken together, represent a monumental breakthrough in the history of these efforts. By now, the paths forged by Luther and countless other Bible scholars are broad and well-trodden. Whole lifetimes of learning and love have been dedicated either to translating scripture into various languages (some very exotic and initially lacking even alphabets) or to distributing such versions to the furthermost points on the planet. Paul asks, "how are they to believe in him of whom they have never heard?" (Rom. 10:14). How indeed? Unless we can hear the witness of scripture *addressing us directly* in a language we can understand, we cannot hope either to know or to trust in God's promise of salvation in Christ Jesus.

Missionaries delight in telling dramatic stories about what happens when scripture portions are placed in the hands of faraway peoples "who hunger and thirst for righteousness" (Matt. 5:6a). They also, if they are honest, have discouraging and sometimes comical reports that document the confusion, misunderstanding, and frustration that frequently result when the cultural context and thought-world of the new convert bears little or no resemblance to the world view and witness of either the Old Testament or the New. Unfortunately, much the same problem exists for twentieth-century, "first-world" Christians whose ancestors were first converted centuries ago!

So You Own a Bible . . . What Next?

Consider the experience of the average (Westernized) young person who has just been given his or her first Bible. Is the race on to read it? Does the mere *possession* of a Bible mean that the insights of scripture will be available to the owner? Ask yourself, what happened to *you* when you were first handed a copy of the scriptures? Did it immediately become a vital force for change and renewal in your life? Although some people can respond positively to this question, the average church member probably cannot. What, then, is the problem? What must the church do *beyond* translating and distributing scripture to make the Bible "fully available" to the laity? *How does the local congregation initiate an active dialogue with scripture in which the Word is both heard and responded to?*

A common response to this problem has been to assume that the Bible is "too difficult" for the average reader and therefore needs to be *simplified*. If this is the case, then we may look forward to increasingly easier-to-read versions of scripture (especially paraphrases) with artificially restricted vocabularies. At some point in the not-too-distant future a version such as the *Good News Bible* (which has a vocabulary level geared to match that of a fifth-grader) may become obsolete because the language will be considered too complex for the common reader to understand! The current attempt to *film* the entire Bible is, at least in part, a response to the general movement away from reading. Does this mean that eventually films and comic strips will be our primary means for making biblical resources available to people? Although it is certainly true that there will always be a need for fresh translations of scripture into timely and intelligible language, *it does not thereby follow that the problem of making biblical resources available to the laity is only or even primarily a problem of "simplification."*

With the many modern-language versions of scripture available to the church today, the argument that the Bible is too difficult, at least in terms of language, has no real foundation. (However, to say that "language" is not the problem is not to say that *literacy skills* may not be! Where basic literacy skills are lacking, the Bible—in any version—is going to prove something of a stumbling block, and the implications of this for Protestant Christianity at least are staggering.)

But what about the ideas and concepts presented in scripture? Even when the words themselves are clear (and of two syllables or less), the ideas they are attempting to express may seem remote, confusing, or simply irrelevant. When this is the case—and it almost always is—the problem is not one of "simplification" but of *clarification* and/or *identification.*

The problem we have with lack of clarity in scripture is generally not a language problem; it is an information problem. The biblical writers lived and wrote in a world vastly different from our own—they had no idea their audience would ultimately include people living anywhere from two to three thousand years into the future. They did not know, as they wrote, that they were producing what first Israel and then the church would someday call "scripture." (Paul was writing letters to co-workers and communities.) Furthermore, when they wrote they assumed a common fund of information and experience—a shared history.

For example, the Gospel writers take it for granted that the reader will understand why tax-gatherers were always mentioned in the same breath with prostitutes and that it would have been profoundly shocking to respectable people for Jesus to call one of them to be his disciple. Nowhere in the gospels does it *explain* that they were chiselers and "quislings"—collaborators with an occupying power and therefore deprived of all political, social, and religious standing within the Jewish community. Through access to standard reference tools—Bible dictionaries and commentaries—we are supplied with this information, which every first-century Christian would have considered common knowledge. Once *we* have this kind of information, many old and too familiar stories suddenly regain the power to shock and amaze us, just as they would have shocked and amazed the people to whom they were first addressed. This is just one of many cases where additional information produces a sudden and very helpful clarification of the biblical material.

And yet clarity is not all that is required for scripture to become a powerful agent of change in the life of Christians and their faith communities. Something may be perfectly clear and stll fail to move us. It is not enough that our scriptures be "clear," they must also address us in a direct, forceful, and compelling way. We must know that what is written there is written *for us*. And so, along with clarification, the church is called to assist the reader in the problem of *identification*. It is not enough simply to distribute scripture, important as that is.

Consider the plight of the Ethiopian eunuch as he returned from Jerusalem to his queen, bearing a precious scroll with the words of the prophet Isaiah. Philip hears him reading aloud and asks, "Do you understand what you are reading?" The answer, in so many words, is "of course not!" The eunuch has no idea *who* the text is about—is the prophet speaking of himself or of someone else? Philip quite naturally seizes the opportunity to interpret the text (from Isa. 53:7-8) in terms of Jesus. There is "good news" in this text for the Ethiopian too. There is a place for *him* in the story, and he is baptized on the spot (see Acts 8:26-39).

What Philip did for the Ethiopian, the church may aspire to do for its entire constituency. But how? How do we recapture the excitement of encountering a biblical text as if for the first time and understanding that, in some way, it is addressed to us? Can the movement of the Holy Spirit be programmed? Of course not. Yet every local congregation can take steps to help create the conditions under which such life-changing encounters with scripture may occur. They can broaden their understanding of what it means both to "translate" and "distribute" the Word of God to the people of God.

34

You Probably Own a Couple of Commentaries Too . . .

Philip's commentary on Isaiah marks the beginning of the church's efforts to make the insights of scripture available to *everyone*, regardless of race, language, or culture, by providing authoritative interpretations of it. The intent of such interpretation is to clarify, to teach, and to exhort to action; and the form in which this interpretation has been most universally available to the laity is, of course, *preaching*. Until the invention of the printing press, preaching (as well as some limited form of instruction or catechesis) provided the only access to scripture for all but a tiny, well-educated minority.

In addition to preaching and as an aid to it, the church has also produced an immense amount of written commentary on the scriptures. These commentaries range from the highly technical, "critical" variety (which often assume a knowledge of Greek and Hebrew) to the purely devotional (often very sentimental, oversimplified, and colloquial). One might logically expect to find a broad range of commentaries that fall between these two extremes, some of which would be highly useful in the context of the local congregation. Unfortunately, this is not the case, although recently, religious publishers have begun to seek the aid of biblical scholars in producing Bible study materials that are both readable *and* reliable—most often in a topical format.[1]

Important exceptions to the rule stated above are some of the *pre*-critical, essentially theological commentaries written by the truly great movers and thinkers in the history of the church. What Augustine, Luther, and Calvin had to say about the Psalms or Paul's Letters (to mention only a few) can still speak forcefully to the church today. The primary obstacle to making use of these outstanding commentators has been the unavailability of relatively inexpensive editions of historical biblical commentary and the church's deplorable lack of interest in the *history* of biblical exegesis.[2]

Those laypersons who discover and make use of biblical commentaries generally find them to be quite helpful and illuminating; but, in practice, the only commentary most churchgoers are ever exposed to is that produced by the major denominations in the form of adult education materials. In the past, many of these materials have tended to patronize the lay reader by simplifying and unjustifiably amplifying the biblical material on the grounds that it was necessary to make the material understandable and "relevant." Some materials are so self-contained that they do not even require the use of a Bible alongside of them! Again, it is refreshing to note that the tide is beginning to turn as more denominational publishers are planning and producing biblical commentary of an increasingly challenging nature.[3]

The assumption is normally made that when such materials fail to move or excite us that the fault is in the materials and that the basic issue is one of improving biblical commentary—of supplying more vital, relevant, and imaginative interpretations. Naturally, poor materials contribute nothing positive and may, in fact, do actual harm; but it is impossible to give an unqualified assent to the proposition that if the church could simply produce more and "better" commentaries, it would then begin to live out of an authentic biblical vision. The problem with all commentaries, even the very best, is that *they do not require any real change in the relationship between the reader and the biblical text.* As in preaching, the (relatively) authoritative interpretation of the commentator is set before the hearer, who, in turn, considers the final result and either accepts or rejects it. In both cases, as a listener or reader, the stance of the layperson in relation to the interpretation is essentially passive and that of a *consumer.* Our thesis is that the scriptures will never be fully available to the laity *until the laity themselves are actively involved in the process whereby commentary or interpretation is produced, that is, in exegetical study that engages the text at a pre-commentary level.*

A Challenge to "Pick Up Your Bibles and Walk!"

What *really* happens between the reading of a biblical text and the fashioning of a valid interpretation? That mysterious and largely uncharted space between text and commentary has always been a kind of no-man's-land for the average layperson. Traditionally, the laity have tended to take one of two positions on this issue: That "space" between text and commentary has either been viewed as a wilderness of temptation which none but the biblical scholar or, at the very least, an ordained minister is equipped to traverse; or, conversely, it has been shortsightedly collapsed by laypersons who claim that the meaning of biblical texts is almost always self-evident and that each Christian is a law unto himself in matters of interpretation. As is so often the case, the reality lies somewhere between these two extremes. There *are* sufficient resources available to the laity to enable them—with the aid of some skills and direction—to "pick up their Bibles and walk" the required distance between text and commentary. On the other hand, *no one* is justified in claiming total self-sufficiency in this still somewhat perilous journey. As in other situations, there is a certain safety in numbers, and the wisest course is for members of a congregation—clergy and laity—to travel the route together, following in the footsteps of the legions of interpreters who have preceded them. (We already profit from these previous efforts in more ways than may be immediately apparent.)

What should happen between text and commentary is exegesis. The problem is, this type of study requires *more time and intellectual effort* than most laypersons (and many clergy) have been accustomed to spending in their encounters with scripture. It involves spending as much time (or more) on the Bible itself (as a "primary" source) as one normally devotes to commentary (a "secondary" source). There are a number of standard reference tools that assist us in making full use of the Bible as a *primary* source—especially a concordance—and that do not "do our thinking for us." Fortunately, it does not require a seminary education to learn how to use these tools in an efficient and systematic way. What does it require?

Engaging a biblical text at the pre-commentary level is a bit like working on an archaeological dig. The exegete must learn to sift through the material in a slow and methodical fashion. This sifting process requires certain skills; it also requires patience and curiosity. Bible study, like so many other enterprises, has suffered terribly as a consequence of the popular demand for instant gratification. Missionaries who devoted their lives to the translation of scripture into foreign tongues found they first had to create alphabets and orthographies and then teach people how to read! Yet the common expectation today is that weekly attendance at a church-school class is all that should be required for the Bible to "come alive." The "Lay it on me, preacher!" attitude must give way to a desire for a more responsible and exacting examination of the Word.

Although this may sound very laborious—like having to learn a new language—the results, in terms of personal involvement with the text, are often spectacular. Strange as it may sound, a substantial investment of time and effort in exegetical study is ultimately exhilarating, not exhausting. Why? *Because it requires a dramatic change in our relationship with the text.* Instead of remaining passive consumers of biblical commentary, lay exegetes can participate in the forming of a very particular but no less authentic commentary of their own. This is because exegesis allows the Bible to have the "first word," while it equips the community to respond in a responsible and faithful manner.

That Sounds Great,
but It Would Never Work in My Church

Given that so many past attempts at incorporating systematic Bible study in church programs have been dismal failures, it is fair—and necessary—to raise questions about both the feasibility and desirability of developing an exegetical approach to the study of scripture in the local congregation. The following objections are the ones most likely to be raised:

1. *The laity have too little background, training, or motivation to succeed at exegesis.* On the whole it is true that the laity, including even experienced church-school teachers and catechists, have an inadequate background in scripture. But if this is true, it is a reflection of a collective ignorance that pervades every level of the church and for which the church must shoulder full responsibility. To continue to neglect the development of the laity in this direction because of a *previous* lack of opportunity is to ensure that this sorry state of affairs will continue. The promise of exegesis is that is always leads to something else beyond. In the pursuit of answers, new questions emerge, new possibilities are explored. Once the motivated Bible student actively engages the text, a learning process is set in motion that

ultimately results in the acquisition of the kind of background we wish all Christians might someday acquire.

But is the laity sufficiently motivated to make the necessary investment of time and energy? This writer's experience has shown that many laypersons are. For the past several years my classes in exegetical method offered to lay men and women of the Baltimore Conference of The United Methodist Church have been popular and well attended. I have taught bus drivers and Ph.D. candidates in the same class, and the single most enthusiastic student I have had to date was a retired longshoreman with a grade-school education. By now the demand for courses far exceeds what one teacher can supply—hence this book! While I have found that many laypersons are actively looking for something of this nature, others who may approach the study process with some apprehension are surprised and delighted when they discover that even a little extra effort yields helpful information and new insights.

2. *The necessary resources are not readily available to the laity.* This objection is less valid now than at any time in the church's history. Characteristically, urban churches have far more resources at their disposal than churches in rural areas and small towns. Public libraries generally make standard reference works available. Where such resources are not available in inexpensive editions, the church must ask itself who is to blame? What are the church's publishing priorities? Has anything been done to sponsor book fairs? If local bookstores do not stock these volumes, it is because there is no public demand for them. Who should be held responsible for *creating* this demand?

3. *The results of lay exegesis are likely to be inadequate or incorrect.* Of course the results of exegesis by beginners will be relatively inadequate when judged by scholarly or professional standards. (The same charge can be brought against the exegesis underlying the typical Sunday morning sermon!) Through continued exposure to scripture, lay exegetes (like preachers) should continue to improve.

The issue of "correctness" poses more of a threat, but, again, our fears in this respect must be seen in the context of the whole history of the church's exegetical work. For example, when we survey the history of exegesis of a single passage, it is clear that its "meaning" can change substantially according to what is called the *Sitz-im-Leben*, or "life situation," of the exegete and the faith community to which his or her work is addressed. No single interpretation of a biblical text can ever be fully authoritative or fully adequate to the needs of the church. Rather, *the whole corpus of exegetical work,* like the canon in relation to a single book of the Bible, serves as a set of controls on the work of any one theologian or interpreter. Likewise, within a local congregation, the exegetical work of an entire study group or committee serves as a control on the individual exegete. I am convinced that the single best defense against bizarre and overly subjective interpretations of scripture is the dialogue that occurs within a *group* of persons who have learned how to read scripture critically and to scrutinize their own responses in terms of the integrity of the texts themselves. If there is anything about which the church is justified in feeling insecure, it is in allowing the laity to remain ignorant of the actual content of scripture. Read in the context of the canon and articulated by the living—and local—body of Christ, the biblical text can be trusted to illumine and evangelize.

4. *Lay exegesis is an encroachment on the preserve of the clergy.* The role of the laity has been undergoing intense reexamination throughout all branches of the Christian church in the last two decades. Protestants have always maintained that the interpretation of scripture belongs to the church as a whole. Interest in the critical study of scripture at every level of the church has blossomed among Roman Catholics since Vatican II. Both Protestants and Catholics are consciously returning to an appreciation of the church as the whole people of God, and both groups speak in glowing terms of the ministry or apostolate of the laity.

As God's people, the laity are being called out of the "darkness" of passivity into the "light" of direct participation in the church's mission. What must be recognized by clergy and laity alike is the futility of speaking of a lay ministry or apostolate *apart from* a solid grounding in an immediate experience of the commissioning Word. No form of ministry, lay or otherwise, can succeed unless it is seen to be firmly rooted in biblical Christianity. An effective lay minister is a knowledgeable and, hence, a *powerful* person.

CHAPTER THREE

Places to Talk:

Creating New Contexts for the Study of Scripture

For from early generations Moses has had in every city those who preach him, for he is read every sabbath in the synagogues.   Acts 15:21

So [Paul] argued in the synagogue with the Jews and the devout persons, and in the market place every day with those who chanced to be there.   Acts 17:17

The Role of Exegesis in Congregational Self-Study: Where Have We Been? Where Are We Going?

The local congregation that wishes to (1) achieve a clearer consensus on the appropriate role of the Bible and (2) develop intentional support for an ongoing dialogue with scripture is advised to undertake a self-study. The immediate goal of such a self-study should be an analysis of the congregation's past and present relationships with scripture, and the ideal setting for it is a church board or council on which all the community's programs and ministries are represented. In any case, people in key leadership positions should certainly be involved along with the pastor and other concerned lay members.

The judicious use of a questionnaire (see sample in Appendix A) will assist in focusing the analysis and discussion; it will also provide a concrete means of measuring change that may take place in the future. Essentially, what the self-study accomplishes is a kind of stocktaking: Where have we been in relation to scripture? Where are we now? Where would we like to be? The outcome of a series of discussions in response to these questions should take the shape of a set of specific goals or priorities in relation to the use of scripture as it applies to the congregation as a whole and to various program areas: church school, small group and committee life, worship and preaching, and so forth.

Initial responses to this sort of self-study are predictable: most church members will view the role of scripture in a relatively partial and privatized way. Within a single congregation the views expressed on the appropriate role of scripture in the life of the church may run the gamut of those outlined in chapter 1 or may reflect a combination of basically conservative or liberal perspectives. In addition, most people will register dissatisfaction with their present grasp of scripture and indicate a desire to "know more *about* the Bible." This need may be expressed in terms of more formal instruction *in church* but is more likely to be expressed in terms of not knowing how to study scripture in a disciplined and effective way *at home*. (Warning: The assumption that scripture should be studied "privately" by the practicing Christian seems almost universal. Since this so seldom occurs in actual practice, to raise even the issue of "Bible study" is to raise the anxiety level of many people!) There will probably be very little awareness of how personal Bible study can be rooted in the experience of corporate worship and witness. Most thinking and discussion will initially confine itself to the more traditional contexts for Bible study: church-school classes, study groups, and private study.

It is important to stress that the analysis of personal and corporate "histories" of encounters with scripture should be dealt with in a leisurely and nonjudgmental way. The purpose of group reflection on the role of scripture in the faith community is gradually to sensitize people to the ways in which their individual lives and corporate identity have *already been shaped* by scripture and to encourage them to plan deliberately for continued encounters at a deeper and more effective level. If the intent is to analyze the use of scripture in all the major areas of corporate life—worship, education, evangelism, pastoral care, and mission—then plans should be made for a long-term study, i.e., from six months to a year.

A self-study on the role of scripture in the life of an individual congregation will not have the impact it should, however, unless the Bible is given an opportunity to speak for itself in the ongoing discussion. Therefore an essential component of and complement to the community's reflection on its relationship with scripture is an intensification of that relationship by means of a careful (i.e., exegetical) scrutiny of biblical texts—texts selected for the light they will shed on the ways in which Israel and the early church understood that same relationship.

The same group that undertakes an analysis of the status quo should also be the group that takes the first step in initiating change. Ideally, each time the self-study group meets, exegetical study should be the *first* thing on their agenda. This is not to be done in a once and for all sense—first we must learn how to study and then we can reflect on our own situation—but in an *ongoing* sense in which study and reflection are continuously linked throughout the entire duration of the self-study. How can this be done?

The simplest method of approach is to plan a series of two- to three-hour sessions in which the first half of each session is devoted to training in exegesis, using either a single biblical text over a series of training sessions or a series of related texts. The study process outlined in chapter 6 lends itself to a leisurely series of lessons in which the various study operations and the tools needed to carry them out can be introduced one at a time, or in stages. If this method is adopted, the group leader should plan on scheduling from six to eight two-hour training/reflection sessions. If at least half of the allotted time is spent learning exegetical method, the group will be reasonably well-equipped to continue their dialogue with scripture in a variety of other congregational contexts. In addition, the training sessions will markedly sharpen the participants' powers of analysis and assist the self-study group in clarifying priorities about the use of scripture in a variety of program areas.

As an alternative to the more gradual method of instruction suggested above, a group might wish to learn the fundamentals of biblical exegesis in an extended, single-session workshop. If the commitment level is high, group members could then be expected to do their own exegesis of a passage prior to the meeting scheduled for self-study, so that the time normally allotted for teaching study methods could be devoted exclusively to discussion of the passage under consideration and its implications for the use of scripture in the local congregation. It should be noted, however, that the average self-study group will probably fare better with the additional support offered by the first method.

In either case, the leader should be prepared for an initial reaction of mild shock and disbelief: "I can't possibly do all that!" For this reason it should be stressed that no one individual has to do a comprehensive exegesis of a passage every time one is called to teach or lead a study; *however,* if even a minimal effort is made to follow the exegetical tasks as outlined, the results will be surprisingly helpful. Very quickly the initial disbelief turns to delighted amazement as people discover that their attempts to examine the text more closely result in a substantial deepening of their appreciation of it. Groups that continue to study and work together will eventually devise efficient and equitable means for sharing study tasks and leadership responsibilities so that no one need shoulder an unnecessarily heavy burden in matters of preparation.

The result of this type of self-study will be ferment and change. What follows is a survey of areas of church life that are most likely to be the locus of change when a community undertakes a direct dialogue with scripture: church school, study and sharing groups, church programs, and preaching and worship.

Sunday Morning: What Do We Owe Our Church School Teachers?

Traditionally, no single group within the church bears a heavier responsibility for "searching the scriptures" than the Sunday school teacher (in Protestant churches) or the catechist (in Catholic parishes). The faith community, which is inclined to expect little of iself in the way of biblical expertise, seems nevertheless to expect a great deal from its volunteer teachers and, consequently, usually has a relatively difficult time recruiting people for this task. Many church members who enjoy working with either children or adults in other settings will politely turn down a request to teach on Sunday morning because they feel so insecure about their own biblical and theological backgrounds—and this is not surprising. In many mainline denominations the average churchgoer knows little or nothing about the Bible.

The failure of church schools to produce biblically literate adults is the result of a combination of factors, not least of which is a long-standing institutional indifference to the issue. Christian education programs for children and adults have tried to be all things to all people. Above all, they have tried to be "timely" and "relevant." In recent decades, a strong emphasis on the Bible has been seen to smack too much of a type of formalized, rote learning that never reaches below the surface and is ultimately counterproductive because it alienates people from the church. Yet the interest in a more "holistic" and integrative approach to Christian education (certainly a positive goal in itself) easily results in a very casual approach to the teaching of scripture. *The problem ultimately lies in the church's failure to perceive their own scriptures as "relevant."* Better biblical preaching will go a long way toward eliminating this misconception, but there is no substitute for a sustained, deliberate, and disciplined encounter with the biblical texts themselves, and if the church school does not provide this type of experience for children and adults, who or what will?

The problem of recruiting and keeping able teachers to teach biblically sound programs is compounded by a number of commonly held assumptions that are both shortsighted and fallacious. The first of these is the belief that unless an individual has had, as a child, a "good" Sunday school background, he or she will not be adequately prepared to teach Sunday school to the next generation. While it is certainly true that previous exposure to an enthusiastic and dedicated role model is a great asset in teaching, the background we acquire as children will not, *in itself,* suffice as appropriate preparation for teaching as an adult. The teacher who best promotes spiritual growth and development in others is the teacher who is requiring the same kind of growth and change in him or herself. No matter what age level we may be working with, our response to the material we teach is shaped by the visions that move us *now*, at our present level of development. Therefore, "training" for effective church-school teaching can never be a once and for all event after which the person may be entrusted with the task of instruction on behalf of the faith community. Rather, training involves an onging (and communal) invest-ment in the spiritual nurture of church-school teachers. The church that makes sound biblical education a priority for its children and adult members must look *first* to providing continuing biblical education for its volunteer teachers—not only by contracting for the occasional services of a professional Christian educator or biblical scholar but also (and more importantly) by supplying the resources and incentive for self-generating and self-sustaining *adult* Bible study within the Christian education committee itself.

The second fallacy that needs to be routed is the assumption that "good materials" will solve the Sunday school "problem." "If we can just find the right kind of materials (biblical or otherwise)," says the church to itself, "then we will have fulfilled our obligation to the church-school teachers and pupils!" Typically, church schools rely on denominational curricula to provide minimum standards of instruction and support for faltering would-be teachers, and no one would argue that good church-school curricula are preferable to poor ones—assuming that some consensus can be reached on what constitutes "good" curricula. Whether the church can or should rely on "good" materials to fill in the gaps in the teachers' biblical backgrounds or provide inspiration and commitment is another question altogether.

Strange as it may sound, our optimism about well-crafted Sunday school materials and our reliance on them can actually function as an *obstacle* to acquiring firsthand knowledge of the Bible. Why? Because most Sunday school curricula consist of attractively printed workbooks, teachers' guides, pamphlets, films, and filmstrips, which, while they are *about* the Bible, tend to get used *in place of* the Bible. Bible stories are "retold" in adult as well as in children's materials as if—somehow—the original writer's words could be improved upon or made clearer through journalistic elaborations. In this way scripture is "mediated" and generally toned down by the latest advances in media technique and by additional layers of interpretation. The prosaic but very significant event of actually handling and learning to "find one's way around" the Bible may, under these circumstances, never occur! Teaching tools and techniques that do not require *direct contact* between the student and the actual biblical text cannot be relied upon to foster biblical literacy in either the teacher or the student.

The "good materials" fallacy is especially pernicious since it rests on the naïve assumption that a teacher's guide can be relied upon to do more than suggest a format or series of activities for a one-hour class. Teacher's guides provide helpful frameworks within which genuine learning takes place; they should not be expected to provide the "meat and potatoes" biblical diet needed by teachers who are, in turn, expected to give their students "the pure milk of the word." What accounts for the failure of the church to place more trust in the power of biblical texts to speak for themselves—especially when so many fine contemporary translations are available?

The answer to this question lies, I believe, in the disturbing tendency of the laity to sell themselves short by underestimating both their own and their children's intellectual abilities. The endless search for "better" materials and interesting activities overlooks the intrinsic power and fascination of the biblical stories themselves. It is assumed that young people must have something interesting to "do" beyond reading, listening to, or responding through discussion to Bible stories: "The kids won't sit still!" In fact, the problem of "interest" needs to be dealt with at the *adult* level first. The real danger is that the *teacher* will not be interested in the material, and this is not surprising. The key to generating interest in learners is developing excitement in teachers, and "good materials" can never take the place of personal involvement with and commitment to scripture in the life of the church. *The single greatest problem facing church schools today is the conviction (on the part of superintendents and teachers alike) that what the teachers need most is an agenda of activities for an hour's worth of time.* In almost every case, the teacher's need is for a clearer understanding of the content and meaning of the Christian faith and a commitment to sharing that faith which is based on a direct and personal encounter with biblical texts.

47

The first step a church can take toward meeting this need is to recognize that it exists and then begin to think creatively about measures that can be taken to support ongoing *adult* biblical education experiences for teachers, parents, and other interested adults. Access to workshops, training sessions in exegetical study and the use of reference tools, along with professionally taught courses in Bible and theology will help immensely. A sustained program of exegetical study related to church-school curricula and conducted by the teachers themselves will do even more. Teachers who have first had the opportunity to struggle collectively with the theological issues in the material they are expected to teach *at their own level of understanding and increasing expertise,* will be in a much better position to extend the same opportunity to children or other adults and to appreciate their questions and problems with the biblical material. Moreover, a teacher who has critically examined the actual biblical text on which a lesson is based will be able to make more effective and discriminating use of the variety of materials and activities available for use in the classroom.

Whatever strategy is adopted to nurture church-school teachers, it is essential that it be seen and carried out as a *collective* responsibility. The quality of learning that goes on in the church school is a direct reflection of the general level of theological expertise and the priorities of the congregation as a whole.

Sharing and Study Groups: Problems and Prospects

The term "Bible study," though it may form an important part of the church school curriculum, is more often suggestive of a relatively small but pious group of devotees who (typically) meet weekly at some time other than Sunday morning. Sometimes but not always clergy-led, such groups make frequent use of Bible study books designed to introduce the reader to a particular book of the Bible, e.g., Genesis or John; or they may simply work their way slowly (sans study helps) through one of the Bible books on a verse-by-verse basis.

Like any small group that meets on a regular basis, these adult study groups have great potential for supporting not only study but genuine fellowship as well. In fact, in many cases, the Bible is used only or primarily as a basis for more personal witness and sharing. These groups serve as permanent reminders to the church community that the scriptures are foundational to an understanding of Christian identity and life-style. The work accomplished in this setting may bear fruit that will benefit the entire congregation and, in many ways, it represents the ideal setting for serious biblical reflection.

Unfortunately, the level of commitment required for membership in such a group is high. Many people who are curious about the Bible and anxious to learn more about it are not yet ready to make such a large investment of their time and energy in Bible study, so they reason, "Why start something I'm not prepared to finish? I'll wait until things settle down a bit . . ." Another problem associated with such groups is their tendency to become ingrown and theologically "cliquish." Often a Bible study group within a congregation becomes characterized by a particular theological stance—usually conservative—which acts to restrict participation to an ingroup of like-minded people. Instead of providing participants with an opportunity to confront and be confronted by a wide range of biblical texts, an ingroup of this description undertakes study that is almost exclusively self-ratifying, i.e., it seeks mainly to reinforce already established beliefs and practices.

Ideally, a weekly Bible study group should offer a setting in which every sector of the community has the opportunity to encounter scripture as a Word of consolation and hope, of challenge and rebuke. When this type of *balanced* encounter does not occur, the group is threatened with becoming a kind of mini-sect within the larger community, attempting to operate at a "deeper" (but essentially a more *privatized*) level than the majority of the congregation. Instead of supporting and undergirding the work of the faith community, ingroup Bible study actually subverts it by providing a haven for the disgruntled.

"Missional" Possibilities for the Committed Bible Student

A core group of committed and enthusiastic Bible students within a local congregation has an important role to play in making the study of scripture foundational to *everything else* the church is doing. In short, such a group has a "mission" to perform, but it will not be able to do this effectively until and unless it makes a conscious decision to *change the basis* on which and for which it meets. This change of basis is best described by the word "conversion."

To be specific, if the members of a weekly Bible study group are in attendance to fulfill what they perceive as their own "personal" spiritual needs, i.e., if they are there *in spite of* everybody else, then their involvement in Bible study is likely to continue their feeling of isolation and ineffectiveness within the larger congregation. If, on the other hand, the committed Bible student is there for the sake of the whole church, i.e., if he or she willingly pursues a greater knowledge of scripture *on behalf of* everyone else, then possibilities for effecting real change in individuals and their congregations will open up. Rather than viewing themselves as a "faithful remnant," such groups would be far more effective if they conceptualized their role as that of "leaven"—i.e., as a hidden agent of transformation that exists to empower and renew the entire "loaf." When this happens the focus is changed from "How can *I* experience better and more fulfilling Bible study?" to "What can *we* do to make the study of scripture foundational to the life of our church community and its witness to the world?"

Thus the Bible study group becomes an effective "mission" group within the congregation when it begins to devote some of its time and attention to the task of strategizing the development of new contexts for Bible study. As committed Bible students, they are in a position to offer opportunities for occasional or short-term study to people who, under normal circumstances, would be unwilling to commit themselves to a weekly study group.

To begin with, the group should take stock of the various church committees and small groups already represented within its ranks. Do any of the group's members also belong to the social concerns committee? to membership and evangelism? worship? music? Any one of these bodies could serve as the setting for a single-session study (or even a brief series of studies) on a topic that would illuminate the committee's special mission in the broader community. How many committee members have a clear sense of the biblical basis of the work they do? How many committee members are aware that such a foundation to their work even exists? Bible students belonging to these groups might begin by volunteering to lead a brief (twenty-minute) study at the beginning of the next committee meeting. Such a study, if well conceived and executed, could have a major impact on the committee's work by sharpening its focus and increasing not only enthusiasm but efficiency as well. Committee members who are, by and large, uninterested in Bible study might find the opportunity for disciplined reflection surprisingly helpful.

Certain groups within the church structure provide rather obvious settings for topical Bible study. The social concerns committee, for example, will find countless biblical references that deal with poverty, hunger, injustice, and political oppression. Similarly, a group concerned with membership and evangelism will find an abundance of material relating to its task; in addition to the obvious and very familiar New Testament passages dealing with conversion, there is a surprising amount of material in the Old Testament that would serve this committee well (for example, the many passages in Isaiah that speak of announcing the "good news" or material in the Pentateuch describing the kind of hospitality Israel is expected to extend to the "stranger").

But what about other groups, especially those with more mundane assignments, such as the finance committee or the board of trustees? Should scripture be expected to inform the work they do? Church members concerned with the material needs of the faith community will find that the heroic efforts of God's people to rebuild Jerusalem and the temple following the Babylonian exile (as described in the books of Nehemiah and Haggai) speak directly to their own predicament and add more zest to their deliberations! Christians who engage in the battle to balance checkbooks and budgets can (with the aid of a concordance) look beyond the familiar passages dealing with tithing and giving and instead do a word-study on "grace," "provision," "abundance," or "supply." Or consider the possibilities for collective spiritual growth should the music committee undertake a study of the theology of the psalms (ancient Israel's hymnbook) as a basis for selecting music for worship!

Although functionally specific groups such as church committees are not the appropriate place for book-by-book study of the Bible, they are precisely the right place for topical studies of the type mentioned above. Topical studies have the further advantage of introducing people to biblical material that they are less likely to encounter in weekly study groups. This is because much topical material is found in books that are seldom selected for thorough study, e.g., Leviticus or Proverbs.

Because topical studies speak directly to the tasks of small groups within the church, they are less likely to be perceived as peripheral or privatized. In theory there is no reason why task-oriented groups should not engage in theological reflection as a basis for shaping policy and guiding practical decisions. Like shared tasks, shared study can be a powerful force for forging bonds between people.

The creative integration of limited Bible study into the program structure of the church is just one of several positive consequences of the effort to strengthen existing contexts for communal dialogue wih scripture. Once a decision has been taken to encounter scripture in a more direct and intentional fashion, more opportunities for dialogue will present themselves—with consequences that are far-reaching and surprising in their impact.

Worship and Preaching: Forms of Communal Support

Although the local church's efforts to improve the use of scripture in its educational and other program areas deserves all the support it can get, the fact remains that these programs generally involve a relatively small proportion of most congregations. It is still true that for the average churchgoer, the *only* time and place of meeting with scripture is the Sunday morning worship service, and the *only* form of biblical commentary to which he or she is exposed is preaching. Therefore the one question no congregation can afford to ignore is simply this: To what extent does the sermon and the rest of the liturgy engage the faith community in an ongoing dialogue with scripture?

The issue of the use of scripture in preaching and other acts of worship revolves to a large extent around different understandings of the nature of preaching. The term "biblical preaching," for example, has become a kind of technical term in professional circles. Why? Isn't *all* preaching supposed to be biblical? If what is meant by biblical preaching is the occasional, offhand reference to biblical texts in support of an argument, then the answer is yes—most preaching is biblical in this limited sense. But that is not what is meant in the field of homiletics by the term "biblical preaching."

It is commonly the case that a pastor decides to preach on a particular subject (e.g., nuclear disarmament, prayer, family values, world hunger). He or she already has some message clearly in mind and so looks for scriptures that will illustrate or support the argument. The starting point and standard by which the texts are judged is the previously established topic and the minister's position in relation to it. This approach to the use of scripture in preaching is referred to as "topical preaching." It is by far and away the most common form of preaching and, in some respects, the most difficult to do well. A good topical preacher is generally a naturally gifted orator who is familiar with the *entire range* of biblical texts on the subject at hand.

In biblical preaching, the process used to prepare a topical sermon is reversed. The starting point is no longer a topic but a text. Preparation for the sermon consists of a careful exegesis of the designated text(s). Out of this study process a topic or controlling idea emerges, suggested by the terms of the text and the questions *it* addresses. In biblical preaching, the Bible is given the opportunity to have the *first word*, even to the extent of setting the agenda for preaching on a weekly basis.

A standard feature of biblical preaching is the use of a lectionary. A lectionary is a schedule of biblical texts designated for public reading according to the church calendar. The use of such a schedule of public readings is nothing new; in fact, it is a very ancient practice that has been traced back to the Jewish synagogue in pre-Christian times. Lectionaries of various types have been in continuous use in the Roman Catholic, Lutheran, and Anglican communions; but for many Protestant churches, especially those in the Reformed tradition, the use of lectionaries represents a departure from tradition. The fact that most mainstream denominations are now turning to the use of a lectionary is due to the groundbreaking work in liturgical reform that came out of Vatican II in the sixties. The expanded, three-year cycle of readings produced originally by and for Roman Catholics in response to Vatican II has been the basis for the development of an increasingly popular ecumenical lectionary that has since been adopted (with modifications) by Episcopalians, Lutherans, United Methodists, Presbyterians, Disciples of Christ, the United Church of Christ, and The Consultation on Church Union. Alongside the development of the ecumenical lectionary, there has been a flowering of interest in the art of biblical preaching. Religious publishing houses have responded to this interest commendably by bringing out a range of lectionary commentaries and study aids designed to assist pastors who undertake preaching from it.[1]

A common (and uninformed) response to the prospect of regularly using a lectionary is to be concerned that it might be too rigid or confining. Actually, the sustained use of a lectionary—*like any other discipline*—is ultimately liberating. Let us examine the ways in which submission to this particular discipline frees churches for more frequent and effective encounters with scripture:

1. *The lectionary liberates the church from limited, personal agendas.* Any preacher, left to his or her own devices, is going to rely on a relatively limited number of favorite and familiar texts that "feel comfortable." When this happens certain biblical writers (e.g., Paul or John) are cited over and over again, while others (e.g., the author of I and II Kings or Ezekiel) are never referred to at all. The sustained use of a three-year cycle of readings forestalls this kind of imbalance, since it requires the preacher and therefore the congregation to deal with a much broader range of biblical material (almost the entire New Testament and a much richer selection from the Old than has ever previously been the case).[2] The lectionary frees the church from the task of "choosing" scripture so that it may once again be *chosen by* scripture.

2. *The lectionary liberates the Word for total accessibility to all sectors of the congregation.* The sustained use of the lectionary allows for a whole new range of well-planned and coordinated

efforts to "preach" the Word in a variety of settings. For example, with a lectionary in hand, a worship committee can design liturgies well in advance and coordinate its efforts with those responsible for selecting music for worship. Lectionary texts may provide the focus for adult education classes or weekly study groups formed to support the pastor through communal exegesis. Lectionary passages may also serve as the basis of study or devotions prepared for committee meetings; and for those who are concerned about developing a disciplined approach to Bible study at home, it is perhaps the ideal solution since it provides an opportunity for the *individual* to make an investment of time and effort that will bear fruit in an enhanced participation in *corporate* worship.

3. *The lectionary liberates the congregation from parochialism by providing for more effective ecumenical cooperation in study and worship.* The Bible, as we have seen, has the potential to unite Christians, but more often becomes a source of division among them. Critical biblical and liturgical scholarship have, since Vatican II, become exciting new arenas of ecumenical cooperation, and the ecumenical lectionary is, in my opinion, the most significant outcome to date of this cooperation. Cooperation at "higher" ecclesial levels is always impressive, but in some ways it is easier to achieve there than at the grassroots. The significance of the lectionary is that, in this case, the cross-fertilization of ideas among professionals signals new possibilities for sharing and exchange at the local level. When most or many congregations are confronting the same biblical texts week after week, it makes sense to develop inter-congregational study groups, either for clergy (who may thus support one another in the task of sermon preparation) or for lay groups that meet in common neighborhoods or places of business.

Pluralistic study groups such as these offer special opportunities and challenges, primarily because the participants do *not* share a common congregational life together. Yet differences in institutional and theological backgrounds need not be an obstacle to satisfying study; if anything, it should work to promote it. Theologically mixed groups are less likely to want to rely on denominationally prepared study materials. For them, the Bible itself is the chief—perhaps only—common denominator, and when this is the case, an agreed-upon strategy for research and discussion (such as the use of lectionary passages) becomes very important. Ecumenical experiences always challenge us to reexamine more closely the foundations upon which our assumptions about the faith rest. A method of lectionary study based on exegetical principles will fulfill this requirement very effectively. (Chapter 5 outlines the specifics of just such a methodology.)

4. Finally, *the lectionary liberates the local congregation for a vital, dialogic encounter with their faith traditions.* There are few, if any, ways of employing scripture in the church that more effectively illustrate the dialogue model described in chapter 1 than the use of the lectionary. Old and New Testament lectionary passages are chosen according to a schema that relates them not only to the church year but also to each other. Over time, a community relying on the lectionary will begin to develop a sound understanding of the ways in which the early church's experience with Jesus Christ and the Holy Spirit either reinforced or challenged sacred scriptural traditions as well as an appreciation of how the church met these challenges. To the extent that these relationships become the subject of careful reflection and discussion, the laity will find themselves empowered to enter into a vital dialogue with their own faith traditions as they are set forth in the Old and New Testaments.

Some Practical Problems for the Supportive Community

Generally speaking, it is not difficult to convince lay members of a congregation that the use of a lectionary offers many new possibilities for opening up a dialogue with scripture. The primary obstacle to implementing such a program is most often a reluctant clergyperson. Therefore, it is vitally important that the laity be sensitive to the issue as it affects the clergy. There are some understandable reasons for this resistance to "submit" oneself to this type of discipline. And let us be clear that the use of a lectionary for preaching is definitely a "discipline"!

The renewed interest in biblical preaching in ecclesial circles is, we must remember, a relatively recent development closely linked to the implementation of the ecumenical lectionary.

Many clergy (*most* clergy), in fact, were trained in seminaries prior to the seventies, when vital fermentation in the field of biblical preaching was beginning to surface. Course offerings in biblical and lectionary preaching are on the increase; yet it is still possible to take courses in homiletics that do not offer instruction on how—or how not—to incorporate scripture into sermons. It is also true that seminarians are still being graduated without ever having taken courses in biblical exegesis. What this means is that many clergy are ill-equipped to deal with passages in an exegetical fashion or to preach from a lectionary.

Although this is a sorry state of affairs, it need not be a cause for despair. There are things that concerned laity may do to promote and nurture the cause of biblical preaching. In the first place, the laity need to take responsibility for letting the pastor know that biblical preaching and the use of a lectionary are important congregational priorities. In the second place, the laity need to offer not criticism but a strong show of support in the form of financial assistance for continuing-education courses in biblical preaching and exegesis. A gift of the lectionary and a set of lectionary commentaries along with up-to-date reference works (such as those listed in the Bibliography) for the pastor's personal library are also appropriate forms of support. Finally, the most effective form of support of all is the gift of the laity's time and personal commitment to what they should learn to conceive of as the *shared* task of biblical preaching. When a pastor expresses an interest in lectionary preaching, the formation of a joint clergy-lay weekly study group whose purpose it is to share the task of exegeting the assigned biblical texts will provide the strongest possible statement of lay support. Even where the pastor expresses no interest in lectionary preaching, the formation of a lay lectionary study group may still make an effective statement about lay interest in and commitment to biblical preaching in general. In either case, the result is a group of well-informed and careful listeners on Sunday morning—people who the pastor knows are anxious to hear the Word proclaimed with integrity and conviction.

CHAPTER FOUR

Learning
the Language:
Mastering the Tools of Biblical Exegesis

Then he opened their minds to understand the scriptures.   Luke 24:45

Learning a new language always takes considerable effort. In its initial stages, the learning process seems tedious and the goal of fluent conversation impossibly distant. The willingness to continue learning after the initial burst of enthusiasm is basically an act of faith—faith that the value of the exchange with the alien other will justify the investment of time and strenuous effort. Unfortunately, many would-be speakers of foreign languages abandon the task long before they are able to string a few sentences together. Impatient for results and afraid of looking foolish, beginners tend to lose sight of the goal long before they have any sense of what the payoff will be.

A vital dialogue with scripture also requires the learning of a new language, in both a literal and a figurative sense. By "language," I do not mean either Greek or Hebrew, although even a smattering of either is wonderfully helpful to the serious student of scripture. The "language" of which I speak is really a set of verbal skills: a small, specialized vocabulary, a grasp of biblical concepts (some of which are expressed in deceptively ordinary language), an appreciation for the limitations of the English language, and the ability to take maximum advantage of the reference tools available. We make the claim that scripture is the "Word" of God. We should not be too surprised therefore to find that biblical exegesis is essentially a *literary* enterprise, requiring and at the same time developing the kind of communication skills all fruitful dialogue requires. Bible scholars, like experts in virtually any field, have developed a technical vocabulary (sometimes referred to disparagingly as "jargon") as an efficient way of communicating with one another. How much, if any, of this vocabulary does the lay Christian need to acquire in order to join in the "conversation"? Or is joining the conversation of scholars a worthwhile goal to pursue? Will the results of biblical scholarship, once interpreted, contribute significantly to the life of the church?

The situation with biblical scholarship should be seen as somewhat analogous to what has happened with the sciences, including medicine. Scientists and doctors communicate with one another through the medium of professional journals. The articles in such journals are often extremely technical and of almost no use to the lay reader who would like to keep up with developments in the field. However, the existence of *popular* journals, such as *Scientific American,* makes it possible for the concerned lay reader to be extremely well informed about new advances in physics, astronomy, and a variety of other scientific subjects. Similarly, the public's growing interest in fitness and preventive medicine is reflected in a proliferation of popular medical newsletters, journals, and even encyclopedias—all designed for the nonspecialist. Through the routine reading of *Scientific American* the layperson gradually acquires a sizable scientific vocabulary, which, in turn, not only facilitates continued reading of that periodical but opens up a variety of possibilities for additional reading and dialogue. The typical science enthusiast has not been known to grumble at having to learn a set of technical terms; he or she is usually anxious to do so. Further, we have all seen how someone facing a medical crisis is determined to learn as much as possible about the threatening disease. Is there any reason why the state of our spiritual development should not be a cause for equal concern?

Unfortunately, there are no journals in the field of biblical theology that can be ranked in quality and content alongside of

Scientific American. (Possible exceptions would be *Interpretation: A Journal of Bible and Theology,* published by Union Theological Seminary in Virginia, and *The Bible Today,* published by the Liturgical Press, St. John's Abbey, Collegeville, Minnesota. As we noted previously, material published in this field—at least until recently—has tended to be either extremely "dry" and technical or sentimental and oversimplified. The lack of intelligent periodicals for popular audiences is disturbing and, I believe, inexcusable. It is a consequence of a relatively modern development: the alliance of most biblical scholarship with the goals and priorities of the secular university. In the pursuit of academic credibility, many Bible scholars have lost all touch with the needs of the church. But the apparent acquiescence of the mainstream church and its failure to require greater accountability—or sensitivity—of its scholars should not be used as an excuse by the laity for not extending themselves in this direction. It is not, I maintain, too optimistic to expect that a biblically informed, theologically articulate laity will be in a position to *demand* access to the results of biblical scholarship through publications that are, at the same time, more relevant and more challenging than what is available now. This handbook is, itself, a response to the growth of this demand at the grass-roots level. It includes (in Appendix B) a brief glossary of selected technical terms that should become a part of the lay Bible student's reading (if not speaking) vocabulary. Intended for on-the-spot reference, the number of these terms is relatively small—yet the access they provide to new worlds of meaning is broad indeed!

Acquiring a Biblical Vocabulary

The lay reader who, in the process of reading, encounters terms such as "apocalyptic" or "eschatology" will be clear about one thing: he either knows or does not know what is being said. Such words are obvious technical terms used to describe biblical material, and they are not normally a part of the average person's vocabulary. But what happens when the lay reader encounters familiar biblical passages that have been translated into plain and simple English? Take the following as an example: "You will be like God, knowing good and evil"

(Gen. 3:5*b*) or "Blessed are . . . your ears, for they hear" (Matt. 13:16). Certainly, there is nothing "technical" about *this* language—surely its meaning is plain enough for anyone to understand!

Had the scriptures been originally written in English we might agree; but anyone who has studied a foreign language realizes how difficult it can sometimes be to translate *meaning* from one medium of expression to another. In biblical literature we often discover that an English word used to translate a Greek or Hebrew term carries only a fraction of the total content the author intended to convey. For this reason, Bible scholars have sought to redefine or elaborate the meaning of many ordinary, nontechnical words that are used by Bible translators when they put the text into English. The results of their efforts are found in theological wordbooks and Bible dictionaries.

The line from Genesis "You will be like God, knowing good and evil" raises several important issues for further word study. The uncritical reader will not recognize this, assuming a common understanding of words such as "God," "good," and "evil." The more alert reader might be aware of a need for further investigation of the terms "good" and "evil," but only a tiny minority of readers will question whether they understand correctly the meaning of the verb "to know" as it is used in this and countless other biblical passages. This kind of skepticism about common understandings of biblical vocabulary is absolutely vital to understanding scripture—*but it must be taught directly and with the aid of theological wordbooks.* It does not come naturally.

One of the finest and most affordable of these wordbooks is Alan Richardson's *Theological Wordbook of the Bible* (published by Macmillan). It contains an entry on "Know/Knowledge,"[1] which informs the reader that the Hebrew verb *yadah* means to "know . . . perceive, learn, understand, have skill"—which is what the English verb "to know" also means. However, the Hebrew verb means that and more: "To know" in Hebrew includes the sense of *a total experience of something.* For example, knowledge of God to the Hebrew is not mere metaphysical speculation "but a recognition of, and obedience to, one who acted purposefully in the world" (p. 122). The knowledge of good and evil held out to Eve by the serpent was therefore something much more momentous than an intellectual apprehension of the nature of these two realities. The wordbook entry goes on to explain that the experiential nuances given by the Hebrew language to the verb are carried over into the Greek New Testament and illustrates this with a reference to John 8:32: "you will know the truth, and the truth will make you free." More than an invitation to exchange one set of beliefs for another, Jesus' charge to "know" the truth is actually a call to conversion. One cannot "know" the truth without receiving the impulse to *do* the truth. Does this mean, therefore, that one may not "know" evil without also experiencing the impulse to *do* evil? A single insight of this kind often radically alters the sense and impact of a familiar passage.

Now take the second example: "Blessed are . . . your ears, for they hear." Again, the uncritical reader would find nothing here to investigate. The more curious student would probably want to know more about the biblical notion of "blessing"; but few indeed are the readers who would question their understanding of words such as "ear" or "hear." Yet this is another set of words requiring special explanation. The wordbook entry for "Hear/Hearken/Ear/Listen"[2] observes that the Hebrews envisioned the body as a unity inseparable from the whole personality, and that while the ear might be the particular organ of hearing, *the entire self was involved in the* act *of hearing.* "There is," the entry continues, "an element of finality and irrevocability once the ears have accepted the message to which they have been opened" (p. 104). It is not a case where the message, once heard, is then deliberated: Shall I accept what I hear or reject it? The reader is astonished to learn that the Hebrew language has no specific word for "obey," and that therefore the verb "to hear" is in practice a synonym for "obey." As the author puts it, "the word of the Lord is uttered that it may be obeyed, and to speak of hearing it is to speak of obeying it" (p. 104). In the light of this new information, Jesus' words "Blessed are . . . your *ears,* for they *hear*" suddenly carry a whole new weight of meaning. Those who "hear" are those who "obey." They respond to Jesus' words by altering all they *are,* all they *do.*

A few discoveries of this sort are generally sufficient inducement to invest in a wordbook. Along with entries for many very common-sounding nouns and verbs (e.g., fulfill, heart, deceit, inherit, time, and desire), theological wordbooks also contain illuminating background information on (1) important theological concepts (sin, grace, revelation, etc.); and (2) biblical personalities and place names that acquired strong symbolic significance in the traditions of the faith community.

A similar but more general and comprehensive resource is the Bible dictionary. The term "dictionary" is really a misnomer for this particular type of reference tool. Most Bible dictionaries are actually small-scale encyclopedias containing alphabetized entries on a vast range of topics relating directly or tangentially to scripture. Like the wordbooks, Bible dictionaries contain entries on theological topics, biblical characters, and place names. Unlike the wordbooks, dictionary entries will include considerable historical, archaeological, geographical, and anthropological data relating to the subject at hand—sometimes at the expense of explaining its theological significance. To illustrate the difference in treatment, consider the entries for "Abraham" in a theological wordbook and a Bible dictionary.

Richardson's treatment of Abraham focuses exclusively on the figure as an important national and religious symbol.[3] Sprinkled liberally with references to both testaments, the wordbook entry points to ways in which the Abraham traditions were used not only by ancient Israel but by the Apostle Paul as he sought to show that faith in Christ should be the primary criterion for entrance into the church. By contrast, the (unsigned) entry in Harper's Bible Dictionary entirely omits the theological significance of the figure of Abraham and concentrates instead on locating him historically, linguistically, and geographically.[4]

Although there are areas of overlap between both types of reference tools—wordbooks and dictionaries—these resources are meant to be *complementary*. One is not a satisfactory substitute for the other. Bible dictionaries do not have entries for those very ordinary-sounding but theologically significant words—like "know" or "hear." Nor do theological wordbooks contain helpful entries on individual books of the Bible, biblical authors, political and religious institutions, and the like.

Since Bible dictionaries are substantial and relatively expensive volumes, a try-out period with copies from the public or church library is recommended. If this is not feasible, compare entries for the same topic (e.g., "Daniel"). You will find that Bible dictionaries, like denominations and local congregations, reflect particular theological biases as well as certain scholastic emphases: Some are relatively conservative, sticking to traditional theories of authorship and dating; others rely heavily on the results of historical-critical biblical scholarship. Certain volumes do better on archaeological and historical topics than others. Individual purchasers generally select dictionaries that contain entries by scholars they consider "trustworthy." A church library ought to be equipped with several such resources, so that borrowers will have access to more than one point of view. A list of wordbooks and theologically representative Bible dictionaries appears in the Bibliography for this chapter (at the end of the book).

The WORD in Words

Systematic use of a theological wordbook and Bible dictionary build respect for the power, importance, and sheer elusiveness of ordinary human language in the biblical enterprise. The student who makes constant use of these resources will find Bible study a rewarding experience rich with challenge and surprise. The student who learns how to use a Bible concordance skillfully passes a kind of "analytical rubicon" and embarks on the path to becoming a grass-roots biblical theologian.

What is a concordance to the Bible? If you have ever seen once, you will wonder how I can possibly make such extravagant claims for it, for of all the available Bible study tools, the concordance is the least glamorous. Consequently few people own one; fewer still know how to use it. This is particularly unfortunate, for *a concordance is the one absolutely indispensable tool for creative and independent study of scripture.*

The word "concordance," in the simplest sense, means

"accord" or "agreement." A Bible concordance is an alphabetized index or word frequency list of all the words (from *Aaron*
to *Zuzims*) contained in the English Bible with citations from
the verses in which these words appear. The first concordance
to the English Bible, compiled by John Marbeck in 1550, was
entitled thusly:

> **A Concordance, that is to saie, a worke wherein by the
> order of the letters of the A.B.C. ye maie redely find
> any worde conteigned in the whole Bible, so often as it
> is there expressed or mentioned.**[5]

People who *do* own and use a concordance tend to use it for
one purpose only: they use it to locate what I usually refer to as
the "mystery" verse—that haunting, half-remembered frag-
ment of a Bible verse they wish to cite in speech, sermon, or
letter but are at a loss to locate. Short of calling the pastor for a
bailout, is there anything one can do to find that verse?

If you can remember only a tiny bit of the precise wording of
the verse the concordance quickly comes to the rescue,
enabling you to find the exact location of the verse in question.
For example, suppose you wished to cite Jesus' words from the
cross, "My God, My God, why hast thou forsaken me?" Instead
of flipping through four different Gospel accounts of the
crucifixion to find it, a quick reference to the concordance will
do in one minute or less what might have taken several (or
many) minutes. The question is: Which of the seven different
words in the quotation should be consulted? As a general rule,
always consult the entries for the least common word in the passage.
"God" is used in scripture so many times, it should be quickly
eliminated from consideration. Words such as "my," "hast," or
"thou" are even more common, and concordances deal with
these either by listing countless, mind-numbing entries or by
dispensing with all but a few of the most memorable
references. "Forsaken" is not quite so common, however. It
represents the best choice in this particular instance for use
with a concordance. A complete or unabridged concordance—
and that is the only kind worth using—will reveal that these
lines appear twice in the Gospels: in Mark's account of the
crucifixion (15:34) and again in Matthew's (27:46). Some

concordances will cross-reference the reader to an identical line in Psalm 22:1—a discovery which might easily elude the reader assuming that the line occurs only in the Gospels. (A glance at Psalm 22 alongside the crucifixion accounts should raise all sorts of questions for the alert student since a number of features in the crucifixion accounts appear to echo lines from Psalm 22—see vv. 7-8, 16, 18.)

For this type of assistance alone, a concordance is well worth owning. After all, how many times can one call on the pastor for deliverance in time of need? The problem is, these simple kinds of tasks are the *most* the concordance is generally asked to perform. Most concordance-users simply have no idea what the possibilities of this remarkable tool really are.

Let us move a step beyond the "mystery verse" function, and look at ways in which the concordance can be made to yield helpful and sometimes very provocative information about the contents of scripture. Take the hypothetical case of an adult class that has become curious about the issue of "sin" as a theological concept and wishes to explore further the witness of scripture on this subject. In particular, the class would like to know what Jesus believed and taught about the subject of "sin." What portions of scripture address this issue directly? Where does one begin the search for information? By far the most efficient way to approach a problem like this is to consult a concordance.

The simplest and the oldest of the still functioning concordances is the (much revised) volume by Alexander Cruden, first published in 1737. Not quite as complete as some of the newer volumes, it is still surprisingly useful, relatively inexpensive, and the least intimidating of all the "complete" concordances. Since it is the most commonly owned type of concordance, I will use it to demonstrate how this particular problem can be solved with the aid of a concordance.

Looking first at *Cruden's* entry on "sin," the class will probably be surprised to find that there are very few references to "sin" in the Gospel accounts. Apparently Jesus had little or nothing to say about "sin" in the abstract! (There is only one reference in Matthew, and that is to Jesus' cryptic remarks about sin and blasphemy against the Spirit. There are nine references to "sin" in John, and, aside from a reference to the "sin of the world" in 1:29, these references speak of sin as a refusal to accept Jesus' divine sonship.) If the group bothers to look a little farther on they will discover that what the New Testament has to say about the problem of "sin" is said primarily by the Apostle Paul. (*Cruden's* cites thirty-nine references to "sin" in the Pauline Epistles.)

Since *Cruden's* does not list all the derivative forms along with the root word, it will be necessary for the class to consult entries for "sins," "sinned," "sinners," "sinning," and so on, in order to confirm their initial conclusions. A little extra effort will show that, even with these additional entries to consider, the Gospel references comprise only a tiny portion of the many biblical references to aspects of sin. For example, there are fewer than a dozen total Gospel references to "sinning" or "sins." The inescapable conclusion of this little exercise is that the Gospel writers did not feel compelled to deal with the subject of "sin" as a theological problem, i.e., sin *per se* is not the issue for them. This discovery should lead the group to question whether the Gospel writers—or Jesus himself—*assumed a common understanding of what "sin" was*—an understanding based on traditions found in Israel's scripture.

The picture changes somewhat when the group examines the entries for "sinner" and "sinners." Suddenly there is a significant number of entries to examine, and, even more interesting, the distribution of these entries is somewhat skewed. Of a total of 29 instances where the word sinner(s) is actually used in the Gospels, 16 (or 55 percent) are found in Luke. The remaining 13 are relatively evenly scattered among the other three Gospels. The Synoptic Gospel references other than Luke (Matthew and Mark) are primarily from accounts that parallel those mentioned in Luke, while the references from John—all located in the story of the man born blind—apply the word "sinner" to Jesus himself! ("Give God the praise; we know that this man is a sinner"—9:24, 25.) What conclusion would the class be likely to draw from this additional information? First, it would seem the Gospel accounts are much more concerned with the *effects* of sin than sin itself and that they show Jesus dealing directly with the effects of sin as he ministers to "sinners." Second, the group might decide on the basis of this preliminary scan that the

Gospel of Luke would be the best resource for a study of the ways in which Jesus dealt with the effects of sin. On the other hand, they might decide that they would be better off sticking to their original goal but studying Paul instead!

To further verify these conclusions, the class would be well advised to scan entries for synonyms for "sin"—words such as "iniquity," "transgression," "unrighteous/ness" or "wicked/ness." If they do, they will discover the same, rather surprising paucity of references in the Gospel writers. One final strategy would be to investigate references for the word "forgive" and its derivative forms. Happily, this turns out to be a subject on which Jesus *did* do considerable direct teaching. *Cruden's* lists a total of 33 references in the Gospels, all relatively evenly distributed throughout the Synoptic Gospels but without a single mention of the word in John! Since, as usual, the Synoptic accounts often parallel one another, the class might well decide to stick with the Gospel of Luke as its basic resource for understanding Jesus' views on the subject of sin/sinners—such as they have been recorded. If so, the study ought to be complemented with some carefully chosen passages from the Old Testament to clarify what kinds of "operational" definitions of "sin" Luke (or Jesus himself) may have assumed.

If space permitted, many such examples could be cited of ways in which a *preliminary* look at concordance entries facilitates group and individual study of scripture. But a warning is in order. Concordance work meant to answer one set of questions almost always gives rise to another set of questions—and so it goes, nor does formal training in biblical studies *necessarily* prepare us for the kind of creative questioning the concordance responds to. The New Testament scholar Harold Moulton explains his attachment to this particular study tool by recounting how a translation assignment with a Tamil New Testament Revisions Committee during World War II and subsequent devotional study opened his eyes to the possibilities of concordance work: "What was borne in upon me increasingly was that it was not my business just to use the Concordance as a tool for my own purposes but to *let it teach me.*"[6] He then goes on to discuss how arranging biblical citations containing key words in logical groupings inevitably reveals a host of important new insights about

68

otherwise apparently familiar material. The exploratory study process he describes is what is known as a "word study." Its purpose is to examine, as fully as possible, the function, range, and development of a given word as it appears in scripture. Word studies are an important aspect of biblical exegesis and are generally done in response to questions raised while working on a particular passage, although they may (as in Moulton's case) be carried out more or less for their own sake or to aid in some technical task. More than any other study technique, word studies are useful introductions to the ways in which the full biblical canon serves to illumine—and often to correct—previous understandings of words we already thought we understood. Furthermore, word studies are really the only means we have for observing and analyzing the sometimes quite unique vocabularies of the biblical writers.

Occasionally someone will attempt a word study only to become discouraged at what seems to be an endless and tedious task. If you *begin* a word study by looking up the first reference cited—and then the second and the third and the fourth—boredom and frustration are certain to set in soon, especially if the list of citations is long. Word study is most effective and efficient when it is approached analytically. *A focus on groupings and patterns should always precede any examination of individual references.* Developed after much trial and error, the analytical word study method described below is the most systematic and efficient means I know of for discovering the marvelous teaching potential of the concordance. It is designed to be used with any of the standard unabridged concordances, such as *Strong's, Young's Analytical,* or *Cruden's*—all of which are concordances to the King James Version of the English Bible. (Unfortunately, concordances to modern-language versions are scarce and almost always too highly priced for the nonprofessional user.) For this reason, it is helpful to have a copy of the King James Version available when doing concordance work. The language of the Revised Standard Version, for example, though very similar to the KJV, contains occasional, sometimes striking differences.

For the sake of illustration, let us suppose that you are studying Luke's account of the walk to Emmaus (24:13-35). The first of the resurrection appearances described by Luke, it is a poignant and powerful story about deep disappointment, amazement, and joy. Speaking of Jesus and his death to the stranger they encounter on the road, the disciples (now sadder and wiser) commiserate: "We had hoped that *he* was the one to redeem Israel" (v. 21—emphasis mine). For what, precisely, were they hoping? What had Jesus done or said to make them think he *would* be the one to "redeem" Israel? And why has Luke selected the word "redeem" rather than "save" or "deliver" to express the content of the disciples' hope? A glance at the concordance entries for "redeem" and derivative forms of the verb reveals that Luke is the only Gospel writer to use this particular word[7] and that he uses it to describe the object of Israel's hope. Another rather surprising discovery is the very infrequent use of the word "redeem" by *any* of the New Testament writers! How is it, then, that Christians so quickly associate the concept of redemption with the work of Christ? One question leads to another with concordance work, and at this point you decide that a word study is in order. The procedure outlined below is, necessarily, done with more precision and detail than the average word study requires. (Percentages are revealing, for example, but not at all essential to good results.) What is important is that the word in question be examined in the context of the *entire biblical canon* and that we learn to look for ways in which *previous experiences become traditions, which in turn are used to interpret more immediate experience.*

Word Study Instructions

Tools: A complete, unabridged concordance (*Strong's, Young's Analytical,* or *Cruden's* preferred); a contemporary English translation of the Bible; a copy of the King James Version; and (for fun) a pocket calculator.

1. Select a word (such as "redeem/redemption") that is central to an understanding of an important theological issue.
   What is your current working definition of this term? ("To redeem" means much the same thing as "to save." Am

70

Anatomy of a Word Study

Major Divisions of the Old Testament ————
New Testament References ------
Books with Significant Word Usage ·········

From *Strong's Concordance*, published by Abingdon.

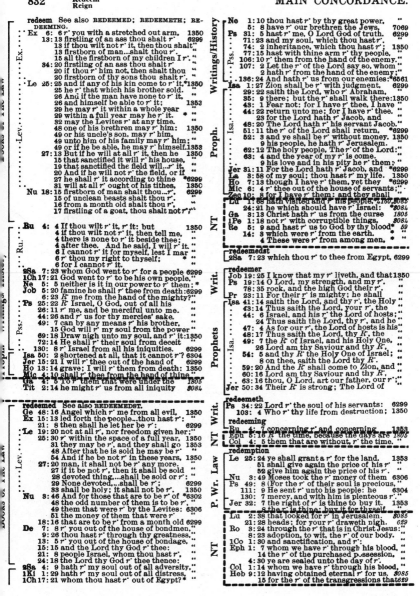

not too sure of the finer distinctions; Jesus and God are both called "Redeemers." Tend to think of it in connection with sin.)

What is the standard secular dictionary definition of this term? (from the Latin, meaning "to buy"; to regain possession by repurchase; to rescue or deliver by paying ransom; "buy off," as a mortgage; make amends or atone for; fulfill. I'm surprised to see that "redeem" is essentially an *economic* term! How did it come to be used theologically?)

2. Scan and analyze the total array of concordance entries for the word, including derivative forms (in this case: "redeem," "redeemed," "redeemedst," "redeemer," "redeemeth," "redeeming," and "redemption").

   a. *Draw a line between the last Old Testament reference for each entry and the first New Testament reference.* Does the word occur significantly more times in one testament than the other, or are the references relatively evenly distributed? (Almost all the references to "redeem" and its derivative forms are from the Old Testament; the number of the New Testament references is surprisingly small—22 out of 160 references total, or 14 percent.)

   b. *Look for patterns or major groupings of the word within the entire Old Testament:*
      —Are most of the Old Testament entries in the Books of the Law? (Yes. Out of a total of 138 O.T. references, 57, or 41 percent, are from the Law, i.e., from Genesis to Deuteronomy.)
      —What proportion of the references are from the Prophets? Does one prophet use the term more than others? (36, or 26 percent of the O.T. references are from the prophetic books. Almost 3/4ths of the prophetic references are from the book of Isaiah.)
      —Does the word appear frequently in the Historical Books or the Writings? Which books from these categories are the most important sources? (A total of 45, or 33 percent, of the O.T. references are from the Historical Books and the Writings. The most important source here is Psalms, which

accounts for almost half—44 percent—of all the references in this category. Next would be Ruth with 17 percent.)

—Is the word important in the Wisdom Literature (Job, Proverbs, Ecclesiastes)? (Hard to say! There are only 4 references altogether, and 3 of these are from Job, which is not really typical of most wisdom writing. Nevertheless, Job 19:25—"I know that my redeemer liveth"—is surely the most famous instance of the word in all of scripture!)

—Does *a single O.T. author* appear to be the major user of the term? (Aside from the legal material in Leviticus, the major user would be Isaiah, specifically 2nd Isaiah, since all but 6 of the 26 references from the book are found in chapters 40–55. Three references are attributable to 1st Isaiah, and 3 to 3rd Isaiah, if one accepts the 3-source theory. Almost as important are the Psalms, but we can't be specific about authorship here. What is interesting is how important the word "redeem," which has such clear economic and legal connotations, is for Hebrew poetry!)

—Are there places in the O.T. where you would expect to find this word where it is absent, or vice versa? (I was surprised to see how often it appeared in Leviticus. I would have anticipated more general use by Israel's prophets. The biggest surprise was seeing how seldom the word was used by New Testament writers.)

c. *Look for patterns or major groupings in the distribution of the word within the entire New Testament.*

—Divide the entries according to the *major categories* of "Gospels" and "Epistles." Are there significant differences in frequency of occurrence? (Although the total number of references is quite small, I would say there is an important difference in frequency of use by Gospel and Epistle writers. Out of a total of 22 uses of the term, only 4—or 18 percent—come from the Gospels.)

—What proportion of the references are found in

the Synoptic Gospels (Matthew, Mark, and Luke) and Acts? (All four Gospel references are from Luke. See above.)

—What proportion of the references are from the Johannine Literature (The Gospel of John, I-III John)? (None.)

—Does the word appear frequently in Paul's Letters? (It appears more frequently here than elsewhere in the N.T. Paul uses forms of the word "redeem/redemption" 12 times. This accounts for 55 percent of the N.T. references.)

—How frequently is the word used by Epistle writers other than Paul (by the authors of Hebrews [relatively few Bible scholars still hold to a theory of Pauline authorship for the Letter to the Hebrews], James, I-II Peter, Jude, and Revelation)? (There is a sprinkling of references here: 3 in Revelation, 2 in Hebrews, and 1 in I Peter.)

—Are there places in the N.T. where you expected to find the word but did not or vice versa? (Overall, I expected to find the word used more frequently by N.T. writers, including—and perhaps especially—Paul.)

d. *What conclusions do you reach as a result of this preliminary scan of both Testaments?* List these conclusions, and make note of *further questions* you have as a result of this analysis. (On the basis of the scan, I would conclude that the word "redeem/redemption" was important for Israel in both a practical/legal and devotional/theological context. "Redeeming" seems equally important to priest and poet and particularly important to the prophet 2nd Isaiah. Any serious study of the term would have to include Isaiah, Leviticus, and Psalms—and probably Ruth too. The much smaller number of New Testament references doesn't necessarily mean that the theme is a secondary one; after all, there is much less material in the New Testament *period*. Paul is certain to have done something creative with it, but what about

Luke? Why, of all the Gospel writers, does he alone use it?)

3. *Examine strategically chosen references, taking note of the larger context in which they appear.*

   a. *Begin with whichever testament has a predominance of the references.* If the references are relatively evenly distributed throughout both testaments, then begin with the O.T. (In this case, we would begin with the O.T. references.)

   b. When working with O.T. references, sample references from each of the major categories: Law, Prophets, History/Writings. As a general rule, it is best to select samples from the books in those categories which are the largest sources of the word. (Samples should include references from Leviticus, Ruth, Isaiah, and Psalms—maybe Exodus, Deuteronomy, and Job as well, simply because these books are very important theologically.) *List those references which are most helpful and revealing. What insights did they yield?*

Books of The Law:

Exodus	6:6	The promise of redemption tied to promise of *election*
	13:13	Redemption of the *firstborn* (context: remembering the slaughter of the firstborn in Egypt and the Passover)
Leviticus	25	Rules for the redemption of family *property* and Israelite *slaves* during the Jubilee year (context: memories of Exodus: "the land is mine; for you are strangers and sojourners with me. And in all the country you possess, you shall grant a *redemption of the land*" vv. 23, 24; emphasis mine.)
Deuteronomy		Moses continues to *remind* both Yahweh and Israel of the Exodus event. Yahweh must not destroy the people he redeemed (9:26). Hebrews must remember that *they were slaves* in Egypt and release their own Hebrew slaves every 7th year (15:15);

similarly, they must treat widows and other vulnerable people with generosity *because of what God did for them in Egypt* (24:18).

History Books/Writings

Ruth 4   Boaz, Naomi's *kinsman*, exercises the *right of redemption* in relation to Naomi's field and her daughter-in-law, Ruth. This ensures the continuation of the deceased husband's line and provides a new family for the widow.

Job 19:25   Despite everything, Job is convinced that he does have a *"redeemer"/vindicator* who will eventually prove his innocence.

Psalms   In almost every case, the word "redeem" appears at the conclusion of psalms which are prayers for *deliverance* from external enemies. The exception is Ps. 130:8, where *redemption from iniquities* is sought for Israel. The psalms recognize that humans cannot deliver themselves: "Truly no man *can ransom himself, or give to God the price of his life, for the ransom of his life is costly . . .*" (49:7-8a).

The Prophets

Isaiah   The prophet emphasizes that *God is, like one's next of kin, a Redeemer of those in bondage* (43:14); God the Redeemer is also God the *Creator* (44:24); furthermore, God's redemptive act has *already taken place*—Israel's *iniquities* have been swept away (44:22-23); God assures Israel of his power to redeem by constantly *calling to mind the revelation of God's power in the 1st Exodus* (50:2); sold for "nothing," Israel will be redeemed *"without money"* (52:3) and *return in joy* to her homeland (51:11).

c. When working with New Testament references, *sample references from each of the major categories of New Testament literature:*

—The Synoptic Gospels and Acts
—The Johannine Literature (the Gospel of John and I-III John)
—Paul's Letters
—Hebrews, James, I-II Peter, Jude, and Revelation

Focus attention on those books in which the word appears most frequently. (Since there are so few N.T. references in this case, all of them should be reviewed.) *List those references which are most helpful and revealing.*

The Gospels

Luke   Israel, held captive in her own land, seeks redemption by a *messiah*. Zechariah believes redemption has once again come to Israel (1:68) and so does the prophetess Anna (2:38). Jesus himself speaks of *immanent redemption* in the midst of *cosmic distress* (21:28); but the *disciples' hopes* and expectations of redemption through Jesus are shattered by the crucifixion (24:21).

The Epistles

Paul   Jesus is himself the long-awaited Redeemer, come in humble form to shame the strong (I Cor. 1:28-31); specifically, it is the *death/"blood"* of Jesus—offered as a free *gift*—which redeems us from *sin* or the "curse of the law" (Rom. 3:24; Eph. 1:7; Gal. 3:15 and 4:5). Purified from sin, the church has become a "people of [Christ's] own who are zealous for good deeds" (Tit. 2:14).

Hebrews   Christ, as the mediator of a *new covenant*, secures an *eternal redemption* for the church with his own *blood* (9:12). The shedding of Christ's blood redeems the called from *transgressions* committed under the *first covenant* (9:15).

I Peter   Christians are exhorted to conduct themselves with scrupulous concern during the

77

"time of [their] *exile,*" *remembering* that they were "ransomed/redeemed" not with perishable things but with the "precious *blood* of Christ" (1:17, 18, 19).

Revelation   The *"new song"* sung by the elders and 4 living creatures praises the *Lamb:* "for thou wast slain and by thy *blood* didst ransom men for God from every tribe and tongue . . ." (5:9). None but the redeemed may learn the new song. Like *firstfruits* set aside for God, they are spotlessly *pure* (14:3-5).

d. Make note of any *new information or insights* yielded by the word study:

—The term is usually applied in relation to situations of slavery and exile (as in Egypt or Babylon).

—Redemption (in the Exodus) is something to be constantly remembered and commemorated. Firstfruits offerings, the Passover celebration, Sabbath and Jubilee Year observances, i.e., rules governing the repurchase of family property and kinsmen in bondage are all ways of remembering the original act of redemption.

—Under Roman rule, Israel naturally dreamed of a new act of redemption. This hope took the shape of a Messiah who would overthrow colonial domination and restore freedom to the state of Israel in a final act of redemption.

—A final offer of redemption is made to Israel but in a surprising and totally unexpected way. In place of political deliverance, Israel is offered freedom from the "curse of the law," i.e., from sin. Jesus freely chooses to pay the cost of redemption by submitting to death on the cross. Jesus' free gift to us is the offer of an "eternal" redemption in the form of a new covenant.

What additional questions are raised by the word study?

—Is redemption a powerful metaphor for a people who have never been enslaved?

—Why should the gift of freedom cost the redeemer so dearly?

—What was there in the tradition that made it possible for the church to accept redemption as deliverance from sin rather than political freedom?

—Why is blood seen to be essential for purification?

—Does the church memorialize the final act of redemption as concretely as Israel sought to memorialize the original act of redemption? What are the words to the "new song" that only the redeemed can sing?

e. Are there any logical or conceptual ways of grouping the references other than by author or literary category?

(Yes. These references might be grouped according to the following categories: God as Redeemer, Christ as Redeemer, Memorials of Redemption or Redemption as deliverance from external enemies, Redemption as deliverance from sin.)

f. Is there any evidence of change, development, or elaboration in the faith community's understanding of the word? At what points do such changes seem to occur?

(The major change seems to be the change in focus from political deliverance or actual enslavement to deliverance from the bondage of sin—a change reflected in almost all of the New Testament references.)

4. When you are satisfied that you have made a thorough study of the references, rewrite and/or expand your definition of the word:

(Scripture uses the word "redeem" to describe a very costly and usually totally unexpected deliverance from physical bondage and/or the slavery of sin.)

5. Reread the biblical passage that led you to do the word study in the first place. How has your research affected your understanding of the passage?

(I now have a much more vivid sense of what the disciples' expectations of redemption must have been. In an experience of political bondage, they would have been remembering the dramatic deliverance at the Sea, the return from exile in Babylon. What else could redemption mean but Israel's complete freedom and an end to foreign domination? Yet this passage suggests that the stranger's words and acts must have forced the disciples both to remember and to reevaluate their scriptural traditions and their experiences with Jesus, the "prophet mighty in deed and word" [24:19]. In the act of breaking bread—itself a kind of perpetual remembering—the stranger is finally recognized as Redeemer. This moment of deliverance from despair is free gift, sheer surprise! The disciples return to their comrades singing the "new song" of resurrection.)

A note of qualification: Formal word study of the type shown above is an extremely effective and disciplined way to study scripture, but—let us be honest—it is also time-consuming and not likely to be a standard feature of everyone's weekly Bible-study routine. Nevertheless, the exploratory attitude developed by word study is something that can be fostered by less extensive, *informal,* on-the-spot word study. Keep a concordance by your side as you study scripture. When your curiosity is aroused by a term, look it up and do a quick visual scan of the entries. You will see *something* that will be of interest, that will raise more questions. Follow through as time permits. Each time you look, you will see more; eventually the need—and the opportunity—for more thorough (and therefore more self-correcting) word study will present itself. (See Appendix C for an abbreviated word study form suitable for regular use.)

The Bible in English: Translations and Paraphrases

Should we need any further convincing of the awesome power of language, we only need look at the history of the English Bible and the bitter feuds new translations often engender. Most of us are aware, for example, that the Revised Standard Version has never been fully accepted by the most conservative wing of the Protestant church, largely because of changes in familiar, specifically theological vocabulary. Very few people are aware that the King James Version was castigated for similar reasons when it first appeared. Changes in religious language, whenever they occur, are emotionally threatening, and this is true whether the motive for change is ideological or simply a desire for greater precision and accuracy. Now, after a surprisingly long and stable period with a single version (the King James for Protestants and the Douay for Roman Catholics), twentieth-century Christians are confronted with a bewildering array of contemporary translations of the Bible in English.

Understandably, most Bible readers feel perplexed or even stymied by the range of choices open to them. It might be reassuring if we could claim that a definitive translation exists—one that is absolutely reliable and readable—but this is not the case. On the whole, we are probably better off without a "definitive" version; otherwise we might be tempted to become entirely too complacent about the issue of what it means to be in dialogue with scripture. Nevertheless, the church (in every age) has a legitimate need for "trustworthy" translations, and by "trustworthy" I mean a translation that *honors* the original biblical texts by reproducing them in another tongue with as much clarity and accuracy as human skill and wisdom will allow. While it is true that some groups are extremely cautious about labeling a new translation or paraphrase as "trustworthy," other more naïve readers assume that any English Bible is virtually interchangeable with any other version, so that "readability" becomes the sole criterion for selection. We need to recognize, then, that if the preservation of biblical texts in the ancient languages is clearly the purview of the academic community, the ultimate fate of the Bible in English will be governed by the purchasing preferences of the Bible-reading public. This is largely a matter of general levels of literacy, literary taste, and intellectual discrimination. Unfortunately, most of the pressure applied by consumers is the result of ignorance about what makes a translation "trustworthy."

To begin with, many Bible readers are not aware of the fact

that of the many English versions available, only some are actually translations from the original Greek and Hebrew texts. One of the most popular Bibles on the contemporary scene, Kenneth Taylor's *Living Bible,* is not a "translation" at all but a "paraphrase," i.e., a restatement in different (presumably simpler) words from an earlier English version—in this case, the "original" was the American Standard Version of 1901. The purpose of a paraphrase is to *clarify* the original. Contrary to what we might expect, an effort at clarification does not generally produce a *briefer* statement. Quite the contrary! When we try to rephrase something, we usually end up elaborating on the original or expanding it. And the more words we add, the more "interpretation" we supply. In theory, translators do not "interpret" texts but attempt to reproduce as objectively as possible what the original author intended to say. In fact, all translation involves an inescapable degree of interpretation, especially when the language of translation is substantially different in structure from the original. The necessity of having to make interpretive decisions accounts for some of the distinctive differences we see in the translation of texts where the meaning of the original is ambiguous. The *Living Bible* has been severely but rightly criticized for containing an unjustifiable amount of interpretive elaboration. Yet every translator, no matter how scrupulously objective, is governed to some extent by a particular theological perspective or academic "agenda." And this brings us to our first rule for Bible readers and students: *Always read the preface to a version of scripture before purchasing or using it!*

The preface to a Bible will reveal a great deal about the assumptions, goals, and biases of its translators or paraphrasers, as the case may be. Yet hardly anyone bothers to consult the preface for this kind of information! Let us look at just a few examples of some popular contemporary versions to see why the preface is often the most "revealing" portion of any Bible:

1. *The New International Version* is a popular and respected new translation from the original Greek and Hebrew texts. What were the goals of the many scholars who worked on it? The preface tells us that they strove for accuracy, clarity, literary quality, and continuity with the long history of the

Bible in English. In addition, we learn that the committee consisted of scholars representing many different Protestant traditions, as well as different parts of the English-speaking world, that they provided for a scrupulous review process by linguists, experts on style, and lay readers. Finally, we learn that this very estimable collection of scholars share one very important commitment, and that is to the "authority and infallibility of the Bible as God's Word in written form."[8] The result of this committee's very lengthy labors is a Bible considered very trustworthy by conservative Protestants. In fact, it is remarkably similar in language and style to the volume for which it is meant to be a more reliable substitute, namely, the Revised Standard Version. The chief differences are, predictably, in matters of theological terminology and in renderings of a few key passages which more liberal scholars would question (e.g., Isa. 7:14).

2. *The Jerusalem Bible* is another very popular contemporary translation widely used by Roman Catholics and Protestants alike. Some Protestants purchase this version without being aware of its Roman Catholic origins and then wonder why the Jerusalem Bible contains biblical books they've never heard of![9] The preface explains that the Jerusalem Bible was originally the work of French Roman Catholic scholars and that the English version was produced by scholars who consulted the French translation along with the original Greek and Hebrew texts. The stated goals of the translators were to serve two needs: the "need to keep abreast of the times and the need to deepen theological thought."[10] While it is not altogether clear what is meant by "deepening theological thought," the Jerusalem Bible is an admirable example of the "flowering" of Roman Catholic biblical scholarship—a development that followed in the wake of Pope Pius XII's encyclical calling for fresh translations from the original languages.[11] It is clearly the intent of this version to open up new and direct means of access to the riches of scripture for a readership whose previous encounters with scripture had been relatively indirect. To this end, the Jerusalem Bible translators have produced a truly outstanding set of notes to accompany the text. Intended to be nonsectarian, they occasionally *do* seem sectarian to the Protestant reader.

3. *The Good News Bible (Today's English Version),* intended originally as a version for readers who learned English as a second language, has been a best seller with native English speakers, much to the surprise of the scholars who worked on it. Without a doubt, the clarity and directness of this translation (as well as its very attractive format) are the basis of its strong appeal; but the average Good News user is quite unaware that the English vocabulary used for this version has been intentionally limited, just as the grammar and syntax have been kept simple. What are the consequences of these decisions? One consequence, of course, is a great gain in clarity and readability. It is difficult to *mis*understand the Good News Bible. But the gain for clarity can also mean a loss of color, richness, and impact in language. Some critics would argue that the poetry in scripture (where simile and metaphor abound) suffers when the vocabulary is artificially limited. Another consequence of working with a limited vocabulary is a move it forces in the direction of paraphrase. Working with fewer *different* words, it is sometimes necessary to use *more* words (in absolute numbers) to express an idea, particularly if the precise word needed turns out to have too many syllables! Fully aware of these consequences, the Good News translators made a "clear" choice in favor of accessibility and unambiguous communication.

4. *The Living Bible*'s preface is a "must read" for everyone who cares about the future of the Bible in English. Kenneth Taylor is to be credited for stating his own particular agenda in plain English, and it's a pity more *Living Bible* users don't bother to read it. In the first place, Taylor states that the *Living Bible* is, as I have said, a paraphrase, explaining that to paraphrase is "to say something in different words than the author used." Taylor's purpose in producing a paraphrase is "to say as exactly as possible what the writers of the Scriptures *meant* and to say it simply *expanding where necessary* for a clear understanding by the modern reader (emphasis mine). Let us reflect, for a minute, on the implications of Taylor's words. The goals of most translators are more modest than Taylor's: Their concern is merely to clarify what the biblical writer *said,* avoiding any unnecessary amplification of the text. When amplification is absolutely necessary it is generally indicated

either by italicizing the added words or by bracketing them. Taylor relies on an inconspicuous system of footnotes to alert the reader to textual amplifications that are sometimes so dubious they amount to actual "emendations" or corrections of the original! For example, Taylor is fond of inserting the word "Christ" into texts where it does not actually appear, because he is certain that "Christ" is what the biblical author "meant." He has John 1:1 read, "Before anything else existed, there was Christ," whereas the Greek text speaks of the "logos" or "word." And even Old Testament texts are reinterpreted for the benefit of the "untutored" reader: Psalm 2 is made to contain the line "the Lord and his Messiah, Christ the King." These liberties are all the more striking in light of Taylor's own remarks about the dangers of paraphrasing. He warns the reader that

> whenever the author's exact words are not translated from the original languages, there is a possibility that the translator, however honest, may be giving the English reader something that the original writer did not mean to say. This is because a paraphrase is guided not only by the translator's skill in simplifying but also by the clarity of his understanding of what the author meant and by his theology. For when the Greek or Hebrew is not clear, then the theology of the translator is his guide, along with his sense of logic, unless perchance the translation is allowed to stand without any clear meaning at all. The theological lodestar in this book has been a rigid evangelical position.[12]

Reader, be advised! Taylor makes it clear that he will not tolerate ambiguity in the text—no matter how "original"—and that a "rigid evangelical theology" will guide him in the matter of clarification, *i.e., amplification.* Anyone who wishes to know with some precision what the biblical texts actually *say* would be well-advised to avoid the *Living Bible,* or at least to supplement it with the use of a standard translation. Serious students of scripture are offended by Taylor's lack of respect for the integrity of the text; personally, I am offended by his lack of confidence in the intelligence of his readers.[13]

The search for a "trustworthy" English version of the Bible ends in the recognition that, with the best of training and intentions, translators will still find honest reasons to differ. Therefore, *the reader's best protection against a certain amount of inevitable bias is to learn to enjoy and profit from a variety of English versions.* In addition, Bible students are well served when they make use of more than one *type* of translation. To illustrate: The most conservative possible type of translation would be an absolutely literal, word-for-word translation. Hebrew and Greek interlinear Bibles achieve this, but they are virtually unreadable and suitable only for reference. A better choice for those who prefer a very literal rendering would be the American Standard or the New American Standard Bibles. These versions are helpful correctives to some of the freer translations but not especially easy to read or understand.

At the other end of the spectrum are the freer translations—the work of scholars who subscribe to the translation principle of "dynamic equivalence." Put simply, this means that, at the cost of literal accuracy, the translator strives to communicate the *conceptual and emotional equivalent* of the original text. The goal is to recreate for the reader, as accurately as possible, the vivid *impact* the original document had on the original audience. The early work of J. B. Phillips falls into this category. Although Phillips worked directly with the Greek texts, he took considerable liberties with them, often adding little flourishes and asides. In the preface to his later, completely revised translation of the New Testament, Phillips explains how the extraordinary conditions of wartime London drove him to take these liberties with the biblical texts and how, years later, he felt compelled to "curb [his] youthful enthusiasms." Yet even with this additional discipline, Phillips continues to be motivated by the same goal that produced the earlier, freer version. "I still feel," he maintains, "that the most important object of the exercise is communication. . . . I want above all to create in my readers the same emotions as the original writings evoked nearly 2,000 years ago."[14] Other contemporary translations that strive for much the same kind of impact include Today's English Version (Good News), the Jerusalem Bible, and the New English Bible.[15]

The best known and, at least until recently the most widely used, of the English versions are those which attempt a compromise position between the goals of complete literal accuracy and conceptual and emotional intelligibility. Commonly the work of an entire committee, rather than a single individual, this type of translation is produced by the principle of "formal correspondence" with the original text. Its purpose is to be both as literal and understandable as possible. Written in customary but relatively formal English, these are the translations we normally hear read from the pulpit: The King James, Revised Standard, and New International Versions, as well as the New American Bible. Although the King James Version is known to contain some inaccuracies in translation, its strengths still outweigh its weaknesses in the minds of many. Among the modern versions, Roman Catholics and liberal and conservative Protestants can all identify at least one of these versions as "trustworthy."

The serious student of scripture should own, *at a minimum,* two different versions of the English Bible: one classified as a "closest equivalent possible" and one as a "dynamic equivalent." For example, you might choose to study the Revised Standard Version alongside the Good News Bible or the New American Bible with the Jerusalem Bible. If vivid, lyrical language is important to you, try pairing the King James Version with the New English Bible. People who break the pattern once with a new translation are usually delighted with the novel perspective this provides and soon anxious to sample more. To be sure, there is nothing to be lost and much to be gained by reacquainting yourself with the scriptures through a fresh and powerful medium.

One final consideration in the selection of Bibles: *At least one of your versions should be a good "study" Bible.* Fine! But what, precisely, makes a Bible suitable for study? Is it a case of the more special features the better? Some Bibles offer so many extra "helps" and "aids" there is relatively little inducement to pay attention to the text! A good study Bible issues an invitation to learn without overwhelming the student with data.

Type size and page layout are more important than you might suspect. Pages with the type set full-width are (in my opinion) preferable to double columns; paragraphing and subtitles (such as those used by the Jerusalem Bible or the New International Version) are exceptionally helpful. More and more, verse numbers are being shown in the margins, rather than in the text. Some people like this, some don't! Do *not* buy a Bible that does not show poetry *as poetry*, and avoid "Red Letter Bibles" like the plague. They add nothing to your knowledge of scripture and mislead many by creating the impression that some parts of scripture are more "important" than others!

Scholarly features, such as annotations, footnotes referring to textual variations and alternate translations are generally very helpful, providing they reflect careful critical scholarship and are not obviously theologically slanted. The same can be said for cross-references, which are often most illuminating. Unfortunately, some Bibles refer to so many of these, the reader is discouraged from ever attempting to examine cross-references. The use of italicized print or quotation marks to show where scripture cites scripture is beneficial, but the reader needs to remember that the placement of these marks reflects an editorial decision; they are not a part of the original texts. Maps and special articles may add to the appeal of a Bible, but most students would do as well or better owning a one-volume Bible dictionary and a separate historical atlas of the Bible. (Some fine Bible atlases are now available in a relatively inexpensive paperback format.) The same goes for abridged concordances often included in Bibles. They are too brief to be of any constructive use. (A *complete* concordance is, as I have attempted to demonstrate, absolutely essential to the study of scripture.)

To summarize: A good study Bible, additional English versions, a complete concordance, a theological wordbook, and a Bible dictionary are the essential tools of the exegete: These are the basic necessities, the foundation on which every personal and church library should be built. But what about the myriad of other tools available? Which of these will aid in the exegetical enterprise?

When You're Ready for More

One of the first supplementary tools I recommend to my students is a "Gospel Parallels." Gospel parallels are ingenious devices that enable the student to study parallel accounts from the Synoptic Gospels side by side. Freed from the necessity of having to flip back and forth from Matthew's version to Mark's and then to Luke's, we can see at a glance where and what the significant differences in the parallel accounts are. A single encounter with this wonderful tool will convince you that it is an excellent investment. (See Bibliography at the back of the book.)

Also helpful, but relatively expensive, are the multi-version Bibles and New Testaments. These volumes, which present several of the English versions side by side, greatly facilitate the first step in biblical exegesis, that of examining the biblical text in more than one translation. Aside from *The Layman's Parallel Bible* (published by Zondervan), I know of no volume that includes the entire Old Testament, and this volume suffers from a relatively restricted and uninteresting choice of translations. *The Eight-Version New Testament* (published by Tyndale House) is an excellent resource.

Bible atlases are important sources of information and fun to use. A good atlas will contain a thorough selection of historical maps in color with additional commentary.

A Word About Biblical Commentaries

Bible students who have discovered commentaries should learn to curb the impulse to reach for them *first*. Commentaries may offer valuable assistance in the study of a text, and for this reason students tend to become much too dependent on them. If a commentary is your *only* resource, then the commentary becomes, in effect, your *only*—and usually very authoritative— teacher. (If this is the case, then one hopes your "teacher" is a good one!) But continued reliance on commentaries will seldom build the kind of confidence and skills needed to do independent *pre*-commentary study—the kind of study that encourages individuals and groups to become full and active partners in a dialogue with scripture.

Used wisely and as one of *several* sources of information, the commentary serves its purpose admirably. Like other re- sources, commentaries reflect the theological perspectives of their authors. For this reason, *it is always safest to consult more than one, and the appropriate time to do this is at the end of the exegetical process and not the beginning.* (A list of one-volume commentaries and popular commentary series is in the Bibliography.)

Biblical Language and the Problem of Sexism

"Inclusive language" is, increasingly, an important and controversial issue for the church. The work of Bible translators has most certainly been affected by criticisms of male-dominated language in the English versions, and although this is not the place for an extended discussion of the merits and weaknesses of the case for inclusive language, I believe a word of warning is in order.

We have seen with the case of the *Living Bible* that the buying public is generally naïve about biblical paraphrases and textual integrity. Many users of the *Living Bible* are not aware when significant departures from the actual biblical text have been made. As a result, they have been seriously misled about the nature of biblical content. The legitimate efforts now being made to revise *unnecessarily masculine* language in the Revised Standard Version are worthy of support. However, attempts by particularly zealous feminist groups to remove all masculine "God-language" through the actual emendation of biblical texts is unjustified and should be resisted. There are places where the Bible is unambiguously masculine in its imagery for God, just as there are places—admittedly fewer—where the imagery for God is feminine. To disguise this is not to "hear" what the biblical text is actually saying, and, *like it or not, we need to listen.* Our *response* to what we hear may, indeed should, be as radical and strong as our experience warrants.

CHAPTER FIVE

Topics of Conversation:

The Problem of Content

They received the word with all eagerness, examining the
scriptures daily to see if these things were so.   Acts 17:11

I t would be difficult to take issue with the assertion that
scripture should be foundational to the corporate worship
and witness of Christian communities. Most congregations
would agree that (in theory) this sounds like a highly desirable
state of affairs. The problem of course is to translate theory
into practice. Practically speaking, *how* does a community
develop a healthy, healing, and challenging relationship with
scripture?

In addition to acquiring resources and learning new skills,
thought must be given to *what* will be studied by whom and in
which settings. The Bible is an immense resource with many
possible points of entry. Does one begin with Genesis 1:1 and
proceed, verse by verse, until reaching Revelation 22:21? Or
should a single book of scripture be selected for study because
it "sounds interesting"?

The problem of content is best solved by a careful
consideration of the immediate congregational context, i.e., by
the special needs and functions of the group that plans to
undertake some form of Bible study. Outlined below are three
basic approaches to selecting biblical content for congregational study: the traditional, one-book-at-a-time approach,
topical Bible study, and lectionary Bible study. Each approach
is presented in terms of appropriate settings, strengths, and
inherent limitations.

The Traditional Book-by-Book Approach

a. *Appropriate Settings:* For many Christians the experience of Bible study has been limited to the traditional book-by-book approach. This may take the ambitious form of beginning with Genesis and working all the way through to Revelation, or it may mean occasionally choosing to study Luke during advent or John during Lent.

The study of an entire book of scripture requires a considerable commitment of time; therefore such studies are best undertaken by relatively stable groups that meet on a weekly basis. Adult or youth church-school classes, weekday or night study groups are normally the most suitable settings for "book" studies.

b. *Strengths.* The study of an entire book of scripture, in contrast to isolated passages, is always an eye-opening experience. When "book" study is done with care and imagination, it is undoubtedly the single best method for developing general "biblical literacy," for the only way to know what is *in* the Bible is to *read* the Bible—and to read it, in most instances, as connected narrative. The biblical narrative in books such as Genesis, Exodus, or Acts is dramatic and gripping. The patriarchal sagas (Genesis 12–50) and the turbulent events of David's reign (II Samuel) engage our imagination and emotions as much—or more—than most modern "page-turners."

To read the individual books of the Bible is to see that the Bible is indeed a "library" or collection of diverse kinds of literature expressing many different theological perspectives. An exploration of the Gospel of John following a study of Mark's Gospel is, quite simply, an astonishing experience. The Jesus John describes is markedly different from the Jesus of the Synoptic Gospels, but this is never really glimpsed when all one reads or hears are selected passages from one Gospel or another. Sustained study of a single biblical author gives the reader an awareness of that writer's own special theological "agenda" and an appreciation for the ways in which this agenda was shaped by previous traditions and critical historical circumstances.

A group wishing to survey the entire Bible faces special

difficulties (which we will deal with below); nevertheless, should they succeed, they will acquire a comprehensive overview of scripture that will serve them well (for *years*) as a context for future studies. This kind of broad survey, which may be handled in more than one way, should be included in the experience of every adult layperson *at least once*. The interested student will want to engage in survey studies periodically.

c. *Limitations*. The study (and not merely the reading) of an entire book of scripture requires time and perseverance. A church class or study group that focuses exclusively on content-oriented "book" study faces the danger of becoming somewhat "academic" in its approach to scripture unless the leader takes steps to ensure that substantial time is devoted to discussing the implications of the material for the local church. The one-chapter-a-week routine is, not surprisingly, *routine*, but this is not the only option available for those who wish to do "book" study. Happily, there are a growing number of fine study books (other than commentaries) available to supplement the biblical text: Robert Kysar's *John the Maverick Gospel* (John Knox, 1976) is a substantive but very readable treatment of important theological themes in the Fourth Gospel; quite different—but also effective—is John Scammon's light-hearted, offbeat study guide for a very "heavy" subject, *If I Could Find God: Anguish and Faith in the Book of Job* (Judson Press, 1974). Significantly, the Women's Division of the Board of Global Ministries of The United Methodist Church publishes a Bible study book annually. A recent effort, *Singing the Lord's Song: Isaiah 40–55* by Bruce C. Birch (1981), is a powerful and imaginative analysis of the experience and images of exile as they apply to the situation of the American church today. *One important caveat:* The use of a study book should never be seen as a substitute for independent exegetical study of representative passages (see chapter 6). When the study book becomes more important than the biblical text, it has outlived its usefulness.

Survey studies of the entire Old and New Testaments are ambitious projects requiring careful planning and skilled execution. Some denominations offer special materials for this type of study (e.g., the United Methodist "Genesis to

Revelation" series), but in every case, the prospect is for an extremely long commitment to a single project, and that can be daunting to even the most enthusiastic students. Yet the commitment of time is only one of several problems connected with survey study. Another serious issue to consider is whether the *order* of the biblical books—as they appear in both the Protestant and Roman Catholic canons—provides the best possible sequence for study. The chart below lists the books of the Old Testament as they appear in the Jewish, Protestant, and Roman Catholic versions of the Bible.

The ordering of the Old Testament books varies considerably between the major traditions; the only areas where there is complete unanimity are the Pentateuch, or the five books of the Law and the list of minor prophets (Hosea through Malachi) also known as "The Twelve." Elsewhere the issue of ordering is confused by disagreements about where to place the collection of books known as "The Writings" and whether or not to include the Apocrypha (or Deutero-Canonical books) separately—or at all. The two Christian canons attempt to place the books of scripture in a kind of "historical" order, i.e., according to the chronology of the events described. The Jewish canon groups the books according to major categories: legal, prophetic, and miscellaneous writings which include poetry, narrative, didactic and some apocalyptic material. None of these groupings arranges the books in the order in which they were written, although the Jewish canon comes closest to achieving this: the three major groupings—Law, Prophets, and Writings—were accepted as canonical in the order in which they appear. (This is not to suggest that all of the material in the Pentateuch is earlier than that of the Prophets; some relatively early biblical material appears in the prophetic books.)

The Old Testament: Comparative Canons

Hebrew Bible	Protestant	Roman Catholic
Law:	*Law:*	*Law:*
Genesis	Genesis	Genesis
Exodus	Exodus	Exodus

Hebrew Bible	Protestant	Roman Catholic
Law:	*Law:*	*Law:*
Leviticus	Leviticus	Leviticus
Numbers	Numbers	Numbers
Deuteronomy	Deuteronomy	Deuteronomy
Prophets:	*History/Writings:*	*History/Writings:*
(former)	Joshua	Joshua
Joshua	Judges	Judges
Judges	Ruth	Ruth
Samuel (1 and 2)	Samuel (1 and 2)	Samuel (1 and 2)
Kings (1 and 2)	Kings (1 and 2)	Kings (1 and 2)
(latter)	Chronicles (1 and 2)	Chronicles (1 and 2)
Isaiah	Ezra	Ezra
Jeremiah	Nehemiah	Nehemiah
Ezekiel	Esther	* Tobit
Hosea	Job	* Judith
Joel	Psalms	* Esther
Amos	Proverbs	* Maccabees (1 and 2)
Obadiah	Ecclesiastes	*Wisdom:*
Jonah	Song of Solomon	Job
Micah		Psalms
Nahum	*Prophets:*	Proverbs
Habakkuk	Isaiah	Ecclesiastes
Zephaniah	Jeremiah	The Song of Songs
Haggai	Lamentations	* The Book of Wisdom
Zechariah	Ezekiel	* Ecclesiasticus
Malachi	Daniel	(Sirach)
Writings:	Hosea	
Psalms	Joel	*Prophets:*
Job	Amos	Isaiah
Proverbs	Obadiah	Jeremiah
Ruth	Jonah	Lamentations
Song of Solomon	Micah	* Baruch
Ecclesiastes	Nahum	Ezekiel
Lamentations	Habakkuk	* Daniel
Esther	Zephaniah	Hosea
Daniel	Haggai	Joel
Ezra	Zechariah	Amos
Nehemiah	Malachi	Obadiah
Chronicles (1 and 2)		Jonah
		Micah
		Nahum
		Habakkuk
		Zephaniah
		Haggai
		Zechariah
		Malachi

*Books identified by Roman Catholics as "Deutero-" or "secondarily" canonical. Note the inclusion of Esther and Daniel in this category.

If one is concerned to read through the Bible in a way that emphasizes conceptual groupings or theological development, then the Jewish order is probably the most helpful, although the placement of the Wisdom books presents problems. Job and Ecclesiastes, skeptical responses to the classical Wisdom thought found in Proverbs and some Psalms, would be better understood if they were read *after* Proverbs rather than before. An alternative to a strict adherence to one canonical order or another would be to allow some flexibility *within* major categories of biblical literature.

Another problem connected with survey studies is the issue of balance and emphasis. Since the Old Testament is so much more extensive than the New, the survey approach usually consigns a group to a great deal of Old Testament study before anything from the New is ever sampled! Some might argue that the church's long neglect of the Hebrew scriptures would justify an "affirmative action" approach to the Old Testament, but this would be an effort to rectify one mistake with another.

Devising a method for studying the entire New Testament is less of a problem; for one thing, there is no variation in the canonical order between Protestants and Roman Catholics, and for another, there is much less material to study! However, the existing order is not ideal for understanding the development of the different theologies represented in the literature of the New Testament, and other strategies should be considered.

For example, if a group wished to study the documents of the New Testament in relative chronological order, they would begin with the Letters of Paul and then proceed to study the Gospels. Since there is serious disagreement among scholars about the dating of the New Testament books, such an arrangement would vary in its details, depending upon the sources consulted; but there is something to be gained by reading the Pauline literature—as the earliest witness to the resurrection and the mission of the early church—*first.*

When studying the Gospels, it makes more sense to begin with Mark, the earliest of the four, than with Matthew, which incorporates large portions of Mark. Furthermore, the Gospel of Luke, written from a Gentile perspective, was intended to be the first of a two-volume history of the life of Jesus and the expansion of the early church. (The second volume, of course, was the Acts of the Apostles.) John's Gospel, markedly different from the other three, is similar in language and spirit to the three brief "letters" of John. Listed below are two alternative approaches to the canonical ordering for New Testament surveys.

Options for New Testament Survey Studies

I	II*

The Synoptic Writers
  Mark
  Matthew
  Luke-Acts
	The Pauline Corpus
	  Thessalonians I and II
	  Galatians
	  Corinthians I and II
	  Romans
	  Philippians
	  Colossians
	  Ephesians
	  Philemon

The Johannine Literature
  Gospel of John
  I-III John	

Pauline Literature
  Thessalonians I and II
  Galatians
  Corinthians I and II
  Romans
  Philippians
  Colossians
  Ephesians
  Philemon
  Timothy I and II
  Titus
	The Roman ("Petrine") Church
	  Gospel of Mark
	  I Peter

	Traditions of Jewish Christianity
	  Matthew
	  James
	  Hebrews
	  Revelation

	The Gentile Perspective Luke-Acts

Letters of the Early Church
  James
  Jude
  Hebrews
  Peter I and II
  Revelation
	The Johannine Literature
	  Gospel of John
	  John I-III

	Miscellaneous Works
	  II Peter
	  Jude
	  Timothy I and II
	  Titus

---

*The order for option II is that which is suggested by Stephen Neill in his excellent introduction to the theology of the New Testament, *Jesus Through Many Eyes* (Philadelphia: Fortress Press, 1976).

Finally, the most serious issue relating to survey study is simply that of attention span. The average student would appreciate greater diversity and more change of pace than a full-scale Genesis-to-Revelation approach is likely to provide. This does not mean that survey studies should not be undertaken; they should. But they are the hardest type of Bible study to do well and are sorely in need of more imaginative treatment and structuring.

d. *Which Books and When?* Groups not involved with survey study are still faced with the question of how best to select biblical books for study. Just how "random" should their selection process be? Are there logical criteria to be followed or guidelines *other than* pure interest and inclination? The answer is yes.

The revival of interest in the ecumenical lectionary suggests new possibilities for coordinating traditional forms of Bible study with what happens during worship on Sunday morning. This is because the lectionary selections from the New Testament include sequential readings from the three Synoptic Gospels (Matthew, Mark, and Luke) as well as from a number of the Epistles. For example, during the first year of the lectionary cycle (Year A), the Gospel of Matthew is read along with Romans, I Thessalonians, and I Peter. In Year B, Mark, James, II Corinthians, and I John are read; and in Year C, Luke, Galatians, Colossians, II Thessalonians, and I-II Timothy. These books are obvious selections for group Bible study when they are used in the appropriate "year."

Unfortunately, the lectionary offers us no help in the selection of Old Testament books, since it does not treat the Old Testament material sequentially but only as it relates directly to themes raised by the Gospel selections (which, as we have said, *are* sequenced). Care needs to be taken, then, to ensure that the books in the Old Testament receive as much attention as those in the New.

One strategy for achieving a good balance between the Testaments is to *pair* books (or substantial portions of books) from both Testaments—either because they complement one another or provide interesting contrasts and developments. Deuteronomy and Romans may be studied one after another as the two major theological treatises of the Old and New

Testaments; Genesis and Acts are accounts of the "first" and "second" creations—i.e., of the cosmos and the church; the Elijah stories in I and II Kings are fruitfully studied in relation to the Gospel narratives about John the Baptist as are the Elisha stories (in II Kings) in relation to the miracle stories recounted in the Synoptic Gospels; Jesus' parables may be studied in light of Israel's Wisdom traditions (e.g., in Proverbs); The Book of Daniel and Revelation are obvious choices for groups interested in the development of Apocalyptic theology; and why not study together the figures of Jonah and Paul (as depicted in Acts)? Both of them required extraordinary forms of persuasion before responding to calls to preach to the Gentiles!

Then again, some Old Testament books may be creatively contrasted with one another, e.g., Exodus and Deutero-Isaiah (Isaiah 40–55), which envisions a "second" exodus out of Babylon, or Job and Jeremiah—great complainers—both of whom dared to contend with God.

Groups that study single books of scripture need to do periodic reviews of their choices to determine whether the full riches of the biblical canon are being sampled. It would be a mistake always to select one of the prophets as an Old Testament book to study, thereby ignoring the Torah, the historical books, or the Wisdom tradition. Similarly, the Epistles should not always be sacrificed to the ever-popular Gospels, nor should Paul's Letters always be allowed to overshadow the smaller but significant collection of letters by other New Testament writers. A balanced approach would be to "rotate" choices from each of the major categories in both Testaments: the Law, the Prophets, and the Writings from the Old Testament, the Synoptic Gospels, the Pauline and Johannine collections, and the miscellaneous Epistles from the New.

Topical Bible Study

a. *Appropriate Settings.* An alternative to the traditional, one-book-at-a-time approach to the study of scripture is the topical Bible study, i.e., the study of a given subject *as it is treated in scripture.* Topical studies provide welcome diversity for

99

classes and study groups that normally use a more traditional approach. In addition, they have the special virtue of speaking directly to the needs of church groups with specific functions: councils, boards, committees, and task forces. (For further discussion of topical Bible study and church program, see chapter 3, pp. 49-52.)

b. *Strengths.* A topical Bible study has the potential for doing two worthwhile things simultaneously: It enhances our appreciation for and knowledge of scripture while at the same time allowing us to focus on a subject of particular or pressing interest and concern. The Bible is such a rich resource that many relevant topical studies may be constructed from it: Suffering, poverty and wealth, childhood and old age, racism, sexism, war and peace, biography, marriage and divorce, and an almost endless supply of theological topics (prayer, faith, election, baptism, grace, sin, etc.) may be the focus of brief or substantial topical studies. In the case of some subjects (e.g., "prayer" or "poverty") a whole series of related topical studies may be constructed for use over an extended period of time by groups with permanent commitments to these special interests.

Topical studies also lend themselves to a variety of treatments or formats, as well as to many possible settings. A series of texts relating to the issue of race might be selected for serious exegetical study by a religion and race commission or a social concerns committee; similarly a building committee might choose to structure brief opening devotionals or reflection periods around a series of texts relating to "Temple," "House of God," and "Build/Building" which committee members themselves had selected. A task force formed to design a series of worship services for a particular season will need to become well acquainted with those portions of scripture around which the liturgical season is based (i.e., the appropriate lectionary selections).

Well-constructed topical studies introduce the student to the full range of relevant canonical material. For example, a study on "prayer" should include material from *both testaments,* as well as from *different types of literature:* treatments of prayer in the narrative books as well as actual prayers from Psalms; Paul's teachings on prayer as well as Jesus'. When this kind of "canonical" approach to topical study is adopted, polarities and tensions in the biblical material become readily apparent, giving rise to more pointed questions and the need for additional, careful reflection. Invariably, this exposure to the breadth and diversity of the biblical vision increases respect for the *complexity* of most issues and appreciation for the continued relevance of scripture as an essential resource for study and decision-making.

An additional benefit of topical Bible study is the opportunity it affords all members of the study group to participate in the planning process. A committee that has spent one session discussing and selecting a series of texts *together* for future study and reflection will find that everyone has a greater stake in the progress and final outcome of the study than would have been the case otherwise.

For groups who wish to use a study book, religious publishing houses are obliging by publishing a long list of attractive titles in topical format, including whole series of topical Bible studies (e.g., Abingdon's Biblical Encounters Series, Westminster's Biblical Perspectives on Current Issues, and Fortress' Overtures to Biblical Theology. See Bibliography for titles in these series.)

c. *Limitations.* Topical studies are normally undertaken because of general interest in a particular subject or issue. If the issue is controversial, then the study is usually intended to assist the congregation in reaching a decision or position on the issue which is faithful to a Christian world view. However, life in a technologically advanced society requires that we deal with a number of controversial issues that are not directly addressed in scripture: methods of birth control and the problems of overpopulation, genetic engineering, organ transplants, complicated and expensive life-support systems, different definitions of "death," or the possibility that homosexuality may be biologically rather than ethically or psychologically determined behavior—to name only a few! But to say that scripture does not directly address an issue is not to say that the Bible has nothing to say to persons and communities who, sooner or later, are called to take a stand. The church, which claims to live by the biblical vision, is obligated first of all to address these issues, and second, to address them prayerfully *in the light of that vision.* Inevitably, what we believe about the nature of God and God's relationship to creation will shape our responses to questions that impinge on the health, freedom, and accountability of ourselves and others.

A different but equally important limitation to topical study arises when the Bible *does* specifically address a given issue. When this happens, people have a tendency to respond in one of two ways, both of which are simplistic and irresponsible. The first response is to consult what "the Bible says" about the issue as if the Bible were a simple collection of indisputable rules. But when the Bible is given the *last* word, then there is no room for discussion and no motivation for study. The second response, equally irresponsible, is to underrate the Bible's authority, dismissing what the Bible has to say on the issue as outdated and irrelevant. This amounts to a refusal to allow scripture to have even a "first" word on the subject. The community that elects to go it alone in reaching decisions on life-shaping issues risks cutting itself off from its root identity and the life-giving "sap" or energy this identification ensures. Properly employed, a topical Bible study allows scripture to have an important and authoritative *first* word on the subject; but until the community has responded to that first word by reflecting on the ways in which it interprets the reality of contemporary experience and vice versa, then no "last" word, i.e., no Spirit-filled conviction that must lead to action, can be experienced or heard.

Finally, it must be stated that topical studies, alone, cannot be relied upon to create a common commitment to a biblical vision of the church and its mission if the Bible has not *already* been allowed to speak with an authoritative voice in corporate worship, preaching, and other forms of study; nor can topical Bible study alone be relied upon to produce the kind of general biblical literacy so sadly lacking in most congregations. In fact, topical studies are undoubtedly *most* effective when undertaken by groups that share a minimal basic competency in scripture. This shared competency is ultimately the best protection against the temptation to rely exclusively on a single biblical reference (or author) as a resource for decision-making.

d. *Guidelines for Designing Topical Bible Studies.* With so many good topical Bible studies by recognized scholars being published (see Bibliography), most congregations may be tempted to use *only* these more substantial treatments of an issue. This would be a serious mistake. Many groups (especially committees and task forces) will fare better with smaller-scale, less ambitious studies which have been tailored to meet either the group's immediate needs or long-term interests.

Selecting a series of topically related texts would seem, at first glance, not too difficult a task; after all, we have concordances (complete and topical) to assist us in finding *all* the biblical references to a subject such as "prayer." But concordances (especially topical concordances) are useful only up to a point; they do not relieve us of the responsibility of making appropriate choices or eliminate the need for artful, imaginative sequencing of the texts selected; nor will every appropriate text contain the actual word (such as "prayer") that identifies the subject under consideration. Ultimately, we are left to rely on our *previous* knowledge of scripture as well as on reference tools when it comes to selecting material for study. There are, however, a few simple guidelines for constructing topical studies which, if followed, will improve everyone's initial efforts.

1. *Strive for a canonically balanced selection of texts.* This means (in most instances) selecting texts from *both* testaments, and wherever possible, from different types of literature *within* the two testaments.

2. *Avoid the tendency to select only brief didactic texts.* For example, when consulting a topical concordance, one finds many references to isolated verses in which a subject is mentioned, often in teaching or preaching context. Paul's exhortation to "pray without ceasing" (I Thess. 5:17) is one such example. The beginner is tempted simply to isolate this one statement without reference to its surrounding context. This is a most unfortunate omission, for Paul is talking about constant prayer as one dimension of a special life-style for Christians awaiting the coming of the Lord. It is a life-style characterized by mutual encouragement and support (I Thess. 5:11), and all those who practice it do so partly because they face the possibility of persecution. A single verse is seldom an adequate text for topical study. The selection process requires that the specific reference always be examined in the immediate context supplied by the biblical writer.

3. *Look for and include relevant narrative (story) material.* Stories can generally be relied upon to prove a point more dramatically and effectively than most other forms of literature. Many biblical narratives may be used effectively in topical studies, even when the connection between the story and the topic is not immediately evident. For example, the story of the young Samuel and Eli is an obvious choice for a topical study on children or youth in the faith community; less obvious are this story's possibilities for making an important statement about old age, but in fact, the trials and tribulations of an elderly priest, Eli, are central to this story and to the youthful Samuel's future development. Similar use could be made of the story of the older woman Naomi and her daughter-in-law, Ruth. At the same time, the book of Ruth could be used equally well in a study on racism, for the faithful Ruth—ancestress of David and Jesus—was not a Jewess but a Moabitess. The stories in Acts about the controversial Gentile mission could be used with profit in a topical series addressing the church's relation to any number of "minority" groups seeking fuller acceptance into the community.

4. *When faced with two equally suitable texts, choose the least familiar.* The justification for this rule should be obvious. The object of topical study—and all study, really—is to broaden and deepen our understanding of a subject. Although there are many times when a fresh look at a very familiar text is really to be desired, topical studies offer the ideal opportunity to present relatively unfamiliar material in a total context that reveals just how useful and instructive the scripture we *don't* know can be!

Shown below is a list of texts selected for a 6-session study by a church building committee. It represents a "first effort" to design a topical Bible study by a student following the suggested guidelines.

BUILDING A CHURCH IN LIGHT OF ITS FUNCTIONS

Old Testament Texts

Session I: Genesis 28:10-22
  (The story of Jacob's Dream. Jacob's "pillow" of stone becomes a pillar in God's house.)

Session II: I Chronicles 28:1-21

(David, not permitted to build the temple himself, commissions his son Solomon to build it according to David's plan.)

Session III: Haggai 1:2-13

(The prophet exhorts the people, busy with their own "paneled houses" to rededicate themselves to building the temple.)

New Testament Texts

Session IV: Hebrews 9:1-22

(How the coming of Jesus changes the way we worship God. *Note:* This session should include some concordance work to show that Jesus and the early church continued to worship in the temple and synagogue.)

Session V: I Peter 2:4-9

(Christ is the "cornerstone" and Christians the "living stones" who, together, are built into a "spiritual house." *Note:* Suggest a word study on "rock"/"stone" which would show that Peter was seen as the "rock" on which the church was built. Have we come full circle from Jacob's "pillow"/"pillar"?)

Session VI: I Corinthians 12:12-27

(The church as the "Body of Christ"—an illustration of the diverse functions the church is expected to perform.)

The student who designed this study did an admirable job of balancing different types of biblical literature from both testaments. We have narrative materials from the Law (Genesis) and the Writings (Chronicles)—even the prophetic passage (Haggai) is "story-like." The Old Testament passages are balanced by an equal number of New Testament selections (although such mathematical precision is not always necessary!). These are essentially theological discourse. The absence of a Gospel passage is unfortunate, but given a six-session limitation, which of these excellent passages would anyone want to omit? (The student's brief notes for sessions IV and V show that she was aware of this omission and concerned to include Gospel material, if only as supporting material for another passage.) All three of the Old Testament passages illuminate the very human dimension of "temple building." In fact, the Haggai passage should probably be expanded to include the material *up to* chapter 2, verse 9. (The first nine verses of chapter 2 comprise one of the most poignant passages in all of scripture: Haggai's description of the crushing disappointment of the elders who remembered the temple in all its former glory with the prophet's reassuring promise that, despite its present humble state, the "latter splendor" of God's house would be greater than the former.) Session V would be strengthened by pairing the passage from I Peter with Matthew 16:13ff. ("You are Peter, and on this rock I will build my church"—v. 18.) Also, Paul's organic image of the church as "body" contrasts sharply with the rock-and-stone imagery of the previous passages. How "different" was Paul's understanding of church from that of the other New Testament writers? Paul uses "building" and "cornerstone" language in two passages: I Corinthians 3:10-17 and Ephesians 2:19-22. Would these be more appropriate here? Or is the contrast deliberately sought? If one of these passages were substituted for the original choice, would the issue of church functions still be addressed?

The ways in which the material is studied or used by the committee may vary considerably. Some combination of individual study and group reflection would probably work best in most situations. But whatever procedure is followed, the committee's work will certainly be affected, i.e., guided and empowered, by a study that directs their thinking to the community's traditional wisdom on "Temple-Building"—wisdom preserved and treasured by "Temple-Builders" for centuries.

RACISM **Selected Texts for a Topical Study***	

I. *Struggle and Reconciliation*
    Genesis 25:21-34;
        32:6–33:11
    Deuteronomy 23:7
II. *The Hated Race*
    II Kings 17:21-34
    Ezra 4:1-3
    Luke 10:25-37
III. *Mixed Marriages*
    Ezra 10:1-5
    Nehemiah 13:23-27
    Ruth 1:1-18; 4:13-22
	IV. *Race and Sacral Purity*
	    Leviticus 20:22-26
	    Acts 10
	V. *Race and Salvation*
	    Matthew 28:16-20
	    Acts 8:26-40
	VI. *The Promise of Freedom*
	    Genesis 12:1-3
	    Galatians 3:26-29
	    Romans 15:7-16

*Designed as part of a training session for persons serving on denominational nominating committees.

Lectionary Bible Study

a. *Appropriate Settings.* The ecumenical lectionary (already discussed at some length in chapter 3, pp. 52-56) is perhaps the most distinctive (yet versatile) of the three approaches to Bible study outlined here. Lectionary selections may be the subject of study for classes and study groups, or the focus for devotions and reflections by committees and boards. (In the case of the worship and music committees, lectionary texts provide an actual agenda.) In addition, lectionary study is ideal for ecumenical study groups in neighborhoods, places of business, and community-wide organizations.

The continuing interest in what is commonly referred to as "personal" Bible study (i.e., study by individuals at home) is, as some denominations are beginning to realize, best addressed by a focus on lectionary texts. Indeed, *why not* encourage the study of scripture at home based on lectionary selections? "Personal" Bible study need not be so private that it bears no relation to what happens when the community comes together on Sunday morning for corporate worship. Ideally, home study of the lections should be supported by a joint lay-clergy lectionary study group that meets weekly to discuss the passages used for public reading and preaching. For many people, such groups create a welcome alternative to regular Bible study classes where the focus may be on long-term study of entire books and the atmosphere considerably more formal.

b. *Strengths.* The most obvious and immediate dividend accruing from lectionary study is a heightened awareness of the role of scripture in worship in general and preaching in particular. A lay-led lectionary study group in a large suburban church made this discovery when it held a formal evaluation after eight weeks of meeting together for an hour prior to scheduled committee and board meetings. Using a "self-anchoring" scale where "5" represented the most positive ranking and "1" the least, the study group averaged a rating of 4.3 in response to the request that they rate the impact of lectionary study on their ability to gain meaning from the Sunday sermon. Over time, consistent use of the lectionary as a basis for study creates an awareness not only of the importance of scripture study to Sunday worship but of the ways in which the Gospel accounts determine the shape of the liturgical year. As one learns something about the strong historical associations connecting particular biblical passages with certain liturgical seasons, a feeling of being rooted in a long, colorful, and vital liturgical history develops.

A second important benefit to lectionary study is an enhanced appreciation for the relevance of scripture to the lives of individual Christians and their communities. This same study group reported that weekly study of lectionary passages deepened their understanding of scripture, giving this issue an average ranking of 3.8. The "givenness" of the lectionary selections ("Here it is; let's see what we can do with it!") implies and sets in motion a different kind of relationship with scripture than most people are accustomed to experiencing. The community no longer selects for itself those scriptures which it already considers "most meaningful" and therefore wishes to hear. Instead, the church is challenged to find meaning everywhere in scripture and to explore more fully the riches of the biblical canon. The net result is an increase in the actual (as opposed to the merely formal) authority of scripture; for while what is said may not always be what we wish to hear, faithful following of the lectionary requires that we listen and respond to even the most difficult of passages. Over time, this change in relationship with the Bible is likely to develop increasingly along the lines suggested by the *active dialogue model* (described in chapter 1). In active dialogue, the authority of scripture is indeed enhanced, but so too is the importance of the community's analysis and evaluation of its own immediate experience. The ability of groups to respond thoughtfully, prayerfully, and confidently to the biblical message will grow as a result of this steady exchange.

In my work of training groups to work with a particular lectionary study method (described fully in the following sections), I found a "hidden" benefit I had not fully anticipated when devising the method. The method I devised reflects the actual structure of the lectionary which correlates Old and New Testament passages thematically, and this forces students to deal directly with the interrelatedness of the assigned passages. For many people, this entailed looking at and coming to understand the Old Testament in an entirely new way, i.e., as a document that relates directly to the revelation of God in Jesus Christ. Evaluations of this methodology have confirmed that lectionary study does not simply enhance one's appreciation of the Bible in general but contributes significantly to renewing interest in and respect for the Old Testament in particular.

One final consideration: Also surprising and certainly important is the potential lectionary study has for reconciliation and church renewal. That this potential exists is evident from the experience of the study group mentioned above. The church in question is a large, prosperous Protestant congregation representing the entire spectrum of theological opinion from "very" liberal to extremely conservative. An unusual and rather tense situation to begin with, the congregation has learned to live with this diversity by institutionalizing "liberal" and "conservative" church-school programs for children and by creating three different adult classes, each bearing the stamp of a particular theological perspective. As a result, there was very little communication between various groups, so when the prospect of forming a new type of Bible study group using an approach that was not easily labeled either "conservative" or "liberal" was considered, a serious effort was made to create a group that would welcome and foster dialogue between diverse elements of the congregation. Co-leaders representing different theological opinions were selected, and participants from all three adult classes and the congregation at large were recruited. To date, the lectionary study group remains—at least in the eyes of some participants— the only forum for theological dialogue between these diverse elements in the congregation. The evaluation ratings in relation to "building understanding among participants" averaged 3.4.

c. *Limitations.* Although the three-year ecumenical lectionary represents a tremendous advance over older and shorter versions, it is still, in some respects a "flawed" reflection of the entire canon of scripture, since its comprehensive coverage applies primarily to the New Testament. There remain many important Old Testament passages that are never included for public reading and preaching. Moreover, the Old Testament passages that *do* appear in the lectionary are there because they have been paired with a Gospel passage on the basis of shared or contrasting themes and images. Old Testament passages do not "set the agenda" for the lections, nor are any Old Testament books read in their entirety, as is the case with many New Testament books.

Lectionary study shares a second limitation with topical Bible study. Although its connection with Sunday morning worship gives lectionary study obvious appeal and personal immediacy, this approach will not supply the same kind of "deep" background that book-by-book study affords. Some would argue that the stimulation provided by lectionary study's immediate feedback compensates for this, but, like topical study, lectionary study is potentially most effective and rewarding when persons using the lectionary already have some background to bring to the study.

Like any approach to the study of scripture, lectionary study should not be the only option available; but it should certainly be available some (if not all) of the time, particularly during those liturgical seasons, such as Advent and Lent, when the lections have long and important historical associations.

Scripture in Dialogue with Scripture

The simplest method for introducing lectionary study is to study *one* of the three lections, preferably the passage selected by the pastor as the basis for the next sermon. With a single passage, any or all of the exegetical study techniques described in chapter 6 may be employed, either at home by individual participants or together with other members of the study group. Depending on the amount of advance preparation, group discussion may focus primarily on the elements needed to understand the passage itself or on the implications of the passage for the life of the community—both aspects need to be touched on.

The single-passage approach to lectionary study is quite satisfactory for many situations; however, it is "lectionary" study in a limited sense only, for the lectionary is not a collection of randomly selected passages to be read or studied in isolation from one another. Quite the opposite! The three-lesson lectionary structure suggests an approach to study and preaching that focuses on the interrelationships between the selected passages, an approach that is essentially "midrashic."

The word *midrash* is from the Hebrew, and it means to "seek out" or "investigate." For centuries *midrash* has been used as a technical term for a particular type of biblical exegesis practiced by Jewish rabbis, including Jesus himself. Midrashic interpretation of scripture is distinguished from a plain, literal sense of a passage by its attempt to probe more deeply into the meaning of scripture. The rules of midrash encourage the exegete to examine a text from every possible angle and thus arrive at an interpretation not immediately obvious to the untutored reader. The primary means by which this is done is through comparing and juxtaposing related biblical texts. Put another way, *midrash* uses scripture to interpret scripture.

In his discussion of Jesus' treatment of scripture in Luke 4:16-30, William Willimon makes the point that Jesus does *midrash* when he uses one set of texts (from I and II Kings) to defend his interpretation of a third text (from Isaiah). In doing this, Jesus sets in motion a dialogue between these texts, and the goal of this dialogue is

> an enriching juxtaposition that results in a meaning that was lacking in the "plain sense" of either original statement but now opens up new levels of meaning for the contemporary community of faith. In this way a familiar text, such as the Isaiah passage, is given new bite by being interpreted through the juxtaposition of two other texts whose authority was admitted. (William H. Willimon, *The Bible: A Sustaining Presence in Worship* [Valley Forge: Judson Press, 1981], p. 76.)

The preacher's goal is always to "open up new levels of meaning," and this is the ultimate purpose of *midrash*. Although the rabbinic rules of *midrash* required a high level of expertise, they also allowed for (and encouraged) a great deal of freedom and creativity. The results of *midrash* were often highly imaginative thematic treatments of biblical texts, sometimes going beyond the bounds of what modern exegetes would consider legitimate.

Lectionary texts, *because they are thematically linked,* are used most effectively in preaching and study when they are set in dialogue with one another, each text providing a unique—and provocative—context for the interpretation of the other. The juxtaposition of two or three related Old and New Testament texts creates an impact, raises questions, and highlights certain emphases, which are not precisely the same as they would be were a single passage alone considered.

The best way to discover the inner dynamics and structure of the lectionary is to observe what happens when one member of a set of three texts is exchanged for another, entirely different text. It is often the case that the lectionary will offer the pastor a choice between two different Old Testament texts, between an Old Testament text and a Deutero-Canonical text, or (in Easter Season) between an Old Testament text and a selection from the Book of Acts.

For example, the United Methodist version of the lectionary (*Seasons of the Gospels,* published by Abingdon) offers the following lections for the Sunday between November 13-19 in Year A. They are readings selected as appropriate for the end of the liturgical year, just prior to the beginning of Advent.

> *Old Testament:* Proverbs 31:10-13, 19-20, 30-31
> or
> Zephaniah 1:7, 12-18
> *Epistle:* I Thessalonians 5:1-11
> *Gospel:* Matthew 25:14-30

Since the Old Testament lections are selected on the basis of themes raised in the Gospel passage, let us look first at Matthew 25:14-30. This is the familiar parable of the talents, in which Jesus compares the coming of the kingdom of heaven to the return of a master who, having entrusted his worldly goods to his servants before leaving on a journey, returns and calls his servants to account. The servants who have been enterprising are rewarded, while the cautious servant, who merely hoards what he has been given without developing it in any way, is judged and punished harshly.

Proverbs 31:10ff. is the famous paean of praise to the "good wife." More precious than jewels, she can be counted on to work tirelessly for the welfare not only of her own family but of the community as well. An early riser, she cooks, supervises the

112

servants, buys real estate and then develops it. She stays up late spinning warm clothing for personal use and future sale; she shares her profits with the poor and, naturally discreet in word, she is absolutely adored by husband and children alike!

Now, if we read the parable of the talents, with the "good wife" passage as a kind of backdrop or context, we shall find ourselves focusing on the accomplishments of the faithful, risk-taking servants who busily put their master's resources to good use. Looking at the Proverbs passage in light of the Gospel text, we will be inclined to view the good wife's industry as evidence of wise preparation, faithfulness, and obedience. Like the enterprising servants, she *deserves* her reward. No foolish virgin she! The sudden arrival of snow and, one presumes, anything else, finds her well prepared. (See verse 21, most unfortunately excluded from the assigned readings. The entire passage—vv. 10-32 should be part of the assigned text.) Taken together, the Gospel and the Old Testament lections emphasize the importance of faithful, fruitful *waiting*.

But what happens if we choose to pair Matthew 25:14-30 with Zephaniah 1:7, 12-18? The prophet speaks only of the time of account-taking, a fast-approaching event he calls the "Day of the Lord" when sudden darkness and devastation on a cosmic scale will shatter the lives of all who are indifferent to God's commands—and this meant just about everyone! Read Zephaniah, and then look again at the parable of the talents. What do you see?

Using Zephaniah's description of the Day of the Lord as a context for reading the parable, we necessarily focus on the event of the master's *return* and not on the time of his absence. We see—and tremble at—the master's scrutinizing of his servants. The terrible, and seemingly unjust, judgment of the cautious servant appalls us. Clearly, the choice of Zephaniah over Proverbs creates a strikingly different kind of "commentary" on the Gospel passage. This striking difference is the *critical* difference on which the axis of the sermon or study should turn.

Since the Epistle passage is sometimes—though not always—selected on the basis of the Gospel themes, it too should be consulted for the light it may shed on the other two lections. I Thessalonians 5:1-11 speaks of the suddenness of the coming of the Lord. Like Zephaniah, Paul envisions this "day" as a time of darkness and sudden destruction, but he is certain that Christians, whom he designates "sons of light and of the day," are not destined for wrath. Awake, sober, and clothed with faith, love, and the hope of salvation, Christians must occupy the interim by encouraging and "building up" one another.

There are obvious connections between Paul's message to the church in Thessalonica and Zephaniah's description of the Day of the Lord. Paul has no doubt been strongly influenced by the prophet's violent and colorful depiction of a time of final judgment. *Yet Paul is equally concerned with what Christians do with their lives while they await the Lord's return.* Beginning with verse 4, the tone of the passage becomes explicitly one of reassurance. Christians know how to prepare themselves for this awesome and much anticipated event. There is a *right* way to wait, and that is with sobriety and mutual support. Paul is, in fact, exhorting the Thessalonians to adopt a life-style much like that of the Proverbial "good wife." The Epistle passage is extremely well-chosen for this set of lections, for it manages to combine the elements of judgment and devastation (as in Zephaniah) along with a concern for the quality of life faithful waiting requires (as in Proverbs).

The Psalm for the day (#128) is unambiguously linked to the Proverbs passage. In contrast to the "good wife," we have here the "happy husband," who, as a reward for his God-fearing practices, is blessed with prosperity, a fruitful wife, and many sons. (The Hebrew text specifies the masculine gender.) His chances for a long, peaceful, and secure existence look very good indeed!

And so, for this particular Sunday the pastor is faced with a clear choice that should ultimately be informed by a prayerful consideration of the needs of the congregation. Either choice is appropriate for this moment on the church calendar, *providing the "commentary" supplied by this particular juxtaposition of texts is respected.* To illustrate: In this context—and perhaps in any—the Proverbs text cannot be legitimately used to show that "woman's place is in the home." Clearly, the point made by the *confluence* of texts selected for this date is that faithful waiting is also fruitful waiting. Industry, enterprise, generosity, and foresight are appropriate modes of action for spouses, servants, and disciples alike! Similarly, Zephaniah's thunderings against corruption in high places and idolatrous religious practices cannot be rightfully considered here *apart from* the prophet's conviction of imminent and ruinous judgment and the almost certain impact this kind of vision had on Jesus' teachings about the coming of the Kingdom. In the last analysis, it is the Pauline passage, with its careful balancing of both elements—those of fruitful waiting and certain fulfillment in judgment—that points the way for the contemporary preacher.

In conclusion, lectionary study is most challenging and effective when it corresponds to the midrashic intent and structure of the lectionary itself. The "thematic" lectionary method outlined below not only takes the basic structure of the lectionary into account but in fact tries to capitalize on it. It may be used with any version of the ecumenical lectionary and is easily adapted for individual use, group study, or sermon preparation. The study options for each lection may be increased (or decreased) as desired, with the exception of the direction to identify and compare key words and themes, since this is essential to understanding the connections between the passages. Consistent use of this method will demonstrate that it is possible to "interpret scripture with scripture" in imaginative yet exegetically responsible ways.

Lectionary Bible Study

I. *Read the Gospel passage first.* The events and teaching material presented in the Gospel passages describe the early church's *experiences* with Jesus of Nazareth and the risen Christ. Since the Gospel accounts were written several decades after the Crucifixion, these memories should also be understood as representing *traditions* about the life, death, and ministry of Jesus.

Study options:

1. Read the passage in more than one *translation*. Make note of any significant differences in wording. Do these differences alter the sense of the passage?

2. Read some of the material that precedes and follows the passage. How does its *literary context* affect your understanding of the passage?

3. Underline *key words or phrases* that identify or point toward theological themes. What problems or issues are raised by this passage? List the key words and phrases in the column marked "Gospel" on your study sheet. (See p. 118.)

II. *Read the Old Testament passage following the Gospel.* The Old Testament was the "Bible" of the early church and, as such, it contains the record of God's dealings with Israel. This record, like that of the Gospels, consists of *traditions that not only describe but interpret Israel's encounters with her God.* The early church made constant use of these vital traditions as it assessed and interpreted its own experiences with Jesus of Nazareth, the risen Christ, and the Holy Spirit. Examine the Old Testament passage *in relation to* the experience described in the Gospel passage. In what ways does it modify or clarify your understanding of what the Gospel passage is "about"? How does the experience described in the Old Testament passage relate to the experience described in the Gospel passage? Do the traditions about Jesus in the Gospel affect your understanding of the Old Testament traditions about God and God's dealings with Israel?

Study Options: Complete steps 1-3 above.

4. *Compare the key words and phrases* underlined in both the Old Testament and Gospel passages. What areas of *overlapping concern* do you find? Make note of these connections.

III. *Read the Epistle passage.* The preaching and teaching material found in the Epistle lections may be understood as a "synthesis" of direct experience (e.g., with the risen Christ or the Holy Spirit) and faith traditions (about the God of Israel). It represents the apostles' efforts to make sense out of their radical encounter with Christ *in relation to* what they had already been taught to believe and expect about the nature and actions of the God of Israel. In many cases, this synthesis is the basis on which the apostle addresses a practical and pressing pastoral problem. The response to the problem may appear to be influenced primarily by immediate experience or by appeal to long-standing faith traditions; often it is a creative blend of both.

Study Options: Complete steps 1-4 above.

5. After comparing and contrasting the key words and phrases for all three passages, *refine and rank the most important common or contrasting themes.* Make a final list of key words for further study.

6. *Consult a theological wordbook/Bible dictionary/concordance* to deepen and clarify your understanding of the most prominent theological themes in this set of lections.

IV. *Reread all three passages* with an eye to the tensions and harmonies present in the "conversation" between them. Listen to, reflect on, and *enter into this conversation yourself.* Taken together, the Gospel, Old Testament, and Epistle lections represent the "faith traditions" of today's church. Just as the early church interpreted its experience of a crucified and risen Messiah in the light of the traditions of ancient Israel, so the church today must continue to reflect on its own immediate experiences in the light of the *full* range of scripture.

V. As part of your reflection on the message of the lections, *read the accompanying psalm.* The psalm, which is selected in relation to the basic lectionary themes, is the appropriate *communal response* to the proclamation of God's word. Where time and inclination permit, the psalm may be studied in the same fashion as the lections, and in any case, it is often a very suitable focus for *personal prayer.*

SAMPLE LECTIONARY STUDY SHEET

Gospel (Matthew 25:14-30)	Old Testament (Zephaniah 1:7, 12-18)	Epistle (I Thessalonians 5:1-11)	Study Summary
The Kingdom is like: journey servants entrusted property/talents according to ability *traded/made . . . more* *dug in ground/hid* *master returns (after a long time)* *settled accounts* *5 talents more* "Well done, good and faithful servant." *set over much* "Hard man" who reaps where *he does not sow* afraid everyone who has, more, etc. slothful, worthless, servant *outer darkness* weeping/gnashing of teeth	*Day of the Lord . . . at hand* sacrifice consecrate guests search (with *lamps*) *punish* Lord will do neither evil nor good goods plundered/houses laid waste *build but not inhabit/plant but not drink* *Day . . . hastening fast* A day of: wrath *devastation* distress *darkness* anguish *ruin* because they . . . sinned blood wealth cannot deliver fire jealous wrath consumed *sudden end*	*times and seasons* *Day of the Lord* *peace and security* *sudden destruction* *no escape* *not in darkness/no surprise* *sons of light/day* *night/darkness/sleep/drunkenness* *day/light/awake/sober* armour (breastplate and helmet) faith/love/hope of salvation Jesus Christ . . . died for us living with Christ encourage/build up each other	primary focus: SUDDEN JUDGMENT Day of the Lord Second Coming/Day of Judgment Everyone who has receives more, etc. darkness and destruction secondary focus: FAITHFUL WAITING prepared/not surprised/awake risk/reaping where you do not sow sons of light *(Note: The themes listed above should be researched with the aid of theological wordbooks, Bible dictionaries, and concordances.)*

Discussion Questions

The preparation of discussion questions for lectionary study should also take into consideration the "conversation" that occurs between the three lections. Listed below are *general*—or model—questions that apply to the five major sections of the study process illustrated above. *They are used most effectively when they are made specific to the passage under consideration.* For example, the question, What traditions about Jesus are preserved in the Gospel passage? might be rephrased, What traditions about Jesus and his teachings are preserved in Matthew's version of the parable of the talents?

Not every type of question suggested will apply to every passage, and if all three passages are to be considered, it will probably not be possible to do justice to more than one or two questions per lection. The important thing to remember is that *the questions used should reflect the ongoing and dynamic relationship between the experience of the faith community* (Israel, the early church, or the church today) *and its faith traditions.*

I. *Model Questions for the Gospel Lections*
    1. What traditions about Jesus of Nazareth/the risen Christ/Holy Spirit are preserved in the Gospel passage?
    2. Does the passage give any clue about the impact of the experience/event described on those who witnessed it?
    3. Does the experience/event confirm or contradict the expectations of the witnesses with respect to God/the Messiah/salvation/revelation, etc.?
    4. Is there any evidence that the Gospel writer is relying on earlier traditions (either from the Old Testament or oral traditions circulating within the early church) to *interpret* that experience/event?

II. *Model Questions for the Old Testament Lections*
    1. What traditions about the God of Israel/the Messiah are preserved in the Old Testament passage?
    2. Does the passage give any clue about the impact of the experience/event described on those who witnessed it?

119

3. Does the passage hark back to or *reinterpret* earlier traditions as a response to some present experience? (e.g., the prophets often made use of the Exodus-Sinai traditions when responding to current crises.)

4. How does the experience described or the tradition referred to speak to the Gospel passage? Does it confirm or contradict it? Does it help to explain the reaction of the witnesses to the event described in the Gospel passage?

III. *Model Questions for the Epistle Lections*

1. What kind of pastoral situation (crisis?) is being addressed by the author of the epistle?

2. What kind of personal (or corporate) experience does the author appear to be drawing on in addressing the immediate situation?

3. Is there any evidence that the author is drawing on a legacy of much older traditional material as he addresses the immediate situation?

4. Does either personal experience or tradition appear more decisive for the author? Is one element ever appealed to at the expense of the other? Is one element ever dispensed with entirely? Or do *both* experience and tradition appear to be reinterpreted in some way as a result of their interaction with each other?

IV. *Reflection Questions for the Church Today*

1. Do the experiences described in any of the lections parallel the experiences of the church today? What has been the impact of contemporary experiences on the lives and beliefs of church members? Do these experiences call into question or confirm received faith traditions (i.e, the witness of scripture)?

2. Do any of the lections provide us with a new basis for interpreting our personal or corporate experiences as Christians?

3. How consciously—and how frequently—do we reexamine our faith traditions (scripture) in the light of our experiences? How much freedom can

we exercise in reinterpreting our faith traditions and still maintain the integrity of the traditions?

4. In what way is the experience of the contemporary church judged by any of the lections? Does the tradition offer the church affirmation or condemnation? How do you expect the community to respond to this judgment?

V. *Model Questions for Reflection on the Psalm*

1. What is the nature of the personal or corporate experience of God described by the psalmist?

2. What traditions about God's dealings with Israel are appealed to by the psalmist? What function does this appeal play? (i.e., is it the basis for an expression of doubt? frustration? confidence? thanksgiving?)

3. In what sense is this particular psalm an appropriate response to the proclamation contained in the lections? (Do they share references to similar traditions or experiences?)

4. Is this psalm an appropriate expression of faith for you and your church at this time? Why, or why not?

CHAPTER SIX

The Bible
Has the First Word:
The Process of Exegesis

What does the scripture say?   Romans 4:3*a*

Beginning Bible students are consistently amazed to discover how much there is to learn about even the shortest, apparently self-evident biblical texts; so unless they are taught a very explicit method for approaching a passage, they are likely to assume that most of what they are reading—because it is familiar—is also relatively obvious in its meaning. This is seldom the case. The beginner needs to be led, step by step, through a process he or she will initially consider unnecessarily thorough. Fortunately, this misconception is quickly corrected. Once the student begins to follow the process outlined below, the delights of discovery provide ample incentive for continuing serious, systematic study of scripture. (See Appendix C for an abbreviated study form of the process outlined below.)

The Initial Analysis: What Does the Text Say?

Although our goal is always to understand the *meaning* of biblical texts, it is a common—and serious—mistake to attempt to interpret a biblical passage before gaining a clear and objective sense of what a given passage actually *says or does not say.*

A. *Consulting Different Versions:* Most of us are careless

readers, especially when dealing with familiar material. We tend to gloss over what we perceive as minor details and then forget them; or we "supply" additional details that are not actually in the text itself. Unfortunately, this type of carelessness may have serious consequences for interpretation. Therefore, and as a *corrective* to this subjective handling of biblical material, the reader should *as a matter of course* consult more than one translation of the passage in question.

A careful reading of a familiar biblical text in another version of the Bible should demonstrate to the student that the material may not be quite as familiar or obvious as was thought. A change in wording often produces subtle but significant changes in emphasis. As an example, let us consider the famous—and very familiar—passage in which Jeremiah prophesies that Israel's God will inaugurate a new covenant with her (Jer. 31:31-34). Although the essential message is the same in each of the versions reproduced below, the *tone* is markedly different in the Jerusalem Bible. (See Table I.)

TABLE I

Jeremiah 31:31-34

Revised Standard Version	Jerusalem Bible
31 "Behold, the days are coming, says the LORD, when I will make a new covenant with the house of Israel and the house of Judah, 32 not like the covenant which I made with their fathers when I took them by the hand to bring them out of the land of Egypt, my covenant which they broke, though I was their husband, says the LORD. 33 But this is the covenant which I will make with the house of Israel after those days, says the LORD: I will put my law within them, and I will write it upon their hearts; and I will be their God, and they shall be my people. 34 And no longer	See, the days are coming—it is Yahweh who speaks—when I will make a new covenant with the House of Israel (and the House of Judah), but not a covenant like the one I made with their ancestors on the day I took them by the hand to bring them out of the land of Egypt. They broke that covenant of mine, so I had to show them who was master. It is Yahweh who speaks. No, this is the covenant I will make with the House of Israel when those days arrive—it is Yahweh who speaks. Deep within them I will plant my Law, writing it on their hearts. Then I will be their God and they

shall each man teach his neighbor and each his brother, saying, 'Know the LORD,' for they shall all know me from the least of them to the greatest, says the LORD; for I will forgive their iniquity, and I will remember their sin no more."

shall be my people. There will be no further need for neighbor to try to teach neighbor, or brother to say to brother, "Learn to know Yahweh!" No, they will all know me, the least no less than the greatest—it is Yahweh who speaks—since I will forgive their iniquity and never call their sin to mind.

Because the Hebrew word *baal* can be translated either as "lord," "master," or "husband," it is possible to portray Yahweh here as a solicitous "husband" or, conversely, as a stern, authoritarian "master." The difference in overall impact is striking!

Sometimes whole chunks of material that are included in one version may be missing from another. A group of Sunday school teachers was studying the story of Philip and the Ethiopian eunuch (Acts 8:26-39). When one of them read the passage aloud from the Revised Standard Version of the Bible some of the others who had been using a different version looked puzzled. One of them asked: "What happened to verse 37? I don't think I heard you read it." In fact, verse 37—Philip's request for a confession of faith prior to baptism—is omitted in most modern translations, since it is considered by scholars to be a gloss, i.e., a later scribal addition. This variation in versions gave rise to several reactions in the group (mostly negative!) and to the obvious questions: Why does the variation occur in the first place? On what basis is it omitted or retained? The issue of whether or not such a profession of faith was a necessary (or original) part of the account formed the basis for further discussion and suggested the need for examining other baptism accounts in the New Testament for purposes of comparison.

(The use of more than one translation is also useful from the point of view of visual impact and literary structure. For example, modern translations usually print Hebrew poetry in the form of stanzas so that it is instantly recognizable as such. The use of paragraphing is of immense help when reading larger amounts of material in sequence, and the addition of topical subtitles—such as those found in the Jerusalem Bible—is especially convenient when trying to select and organize material for study.)

B. *Paraphrasing the Passage:* Once the wording of a text has been examined as thoroughly as possible, the student should attempt a brief paraphrase. Far from being mere busy work, the construction of an accurate, unvarnished paraphrase is probably the single most effective means there is for arriving at an *objective* understanding of what the text really does or does not *say*. The restatement of something in a few, well-chosen words is not easy. The tendency is always to *expand* the original by elaborating on it. Instead of restating, we generally *interpret* or "explain." But an expanded or interpretive paraphrase simply clouds the issues at this stage of the study process. The point of biblical exegesis is to *discover* meaning and not to impose it. For this reason, it is important that the individual student or group resist the urge to conjecture about the text's meaning until after further study.

Table II reproduces two *initial* paraphrases of Jeremiah 31:31-34. When time permits, students should share their efforts with one another. The wide variations in emphasis in these early responses to the passage as well as a certain amount of interpretive expansion uncovered in the process of sharing provide instructive—and rather sobering—object lessons on just how *un*self-evident the sense of a biblical text can be! In addition, it is a good idea to keep these initial paraphrases for further reference. They are often an effective means for gauging changes in perspective that occur as a result of further study.

TABLE II

Initial Paraphrases of Jeremiah 31:31-34

Listen, the time is drawing near, says the Lord, when I will make a new agreement with Israel and Judah which will be different from the old agreement I made with their parents when I led them out of Egypt. They broke	Pay attention! The time will soon come when I will create a new relationship with the kingdoms of Israel and Judah; it will not be like the former relationship, the one I made with their progenitors when I rescued them from

this agreement. I was their guardian, says the Lord. The new agreement which I will make with Israel will be this: I will place my Word within them, and on their hearts; I will be their Lord and they my people. They will not have to say to each other, "Acknowledge God" because each and every one of them will acknowledge me. I will forgive their wrongdoing and forget their sins.

Egypt. They did not keep faith with that relationship, even though I "married" myself to them, says Yahweh. But here is the relationship which I shall form with the people of Israel when the time comes, says Yahweh: I will make my commandments a part of their innermost being, and I will engrave it on their souls; and I will belong to them and they will belong to me. It will no longer be necessary to instruct anyone about who I am and how to understand me, for everyone will understand me, from the wisest persons to the simplest; for I will no longer hold their evil ways against them, and I will forget all their misdeeds.

Context Questions: What Does the Text Mean?

A. *The Congregational Context:* The issues of where, when, why, and by whom a biblical passage is being studied are all important factors in determining what questions will be asked of the text. Bible students should always be conscious of the particular social or organizational context for study. Most often this context is a congregational or "ecclesial" one. A particular group within the church with particular needs and interests undertakes the study of scripture. This group may be a class, committee, house church, study fellowship, or church school teachers and catechists. Whoever they may be, they will certainly have their own agenda, and this agenda provides the most immediate—and certainly the most compelling—context for study. Although this immediate need or interest is often lost sight of in the actual study and discussion process, it inevitably influences the process of selection that always occurs in research and discussion. An awareness of this congregational context or immediate agenda will do two things: It will serve as a corrective for biased readings of biblical texts and, at the same time, it will make for more efficient use of time and reference tools.

To illustrate this, let us return to the group of Sunday school teachers who were reading the story of Philip and the Ethiopian eunuch. Their interest in the question of a profession of faith prior to baptism followed naturally from their concern with Christian formation. Similarly, they were interested in Philip's role as an interpreter of scripture, and so a closer look at that "puzzling" passage from Isaiah which the Ethiopian eunuch was reading might well be included within the focus of their study. Such conscious pre-selection of a particular emphasis in study of a given text is certainly warranted *provided students realize that the selection must inevitably slant the outcome,* at least to some extent. Consider, for example, how different the approach to this passage might be, both in terms of research and the selection of discussion questions, if the group studying the passage was concerned with the issue of ethnic minorities in the church!

B. *The Literary Context:* Any particular biblical passage chosen for study is also part of a larger collection of material, and the position it occupies in that collection provides us with a broader (and therefore more secure) framework for understanding what the passage may have meant originally both to its author and the community for which the author wrote. Therefore, *and as a matter of course,* students should always read some of the material that immediately precedes and follows the passage in question. The broader literary context of a text almost always sharpens its focus for us and provides important clues for its interpretation.

Let us look again at the popular passage from Jeremiah (31:31-34). How many of those who find its message "inspiring" know anything at all about the circumstances surrounding its pronouncement: How often is it seen as one of a series of messages of hope and restoration offered to a nation that had suffered a shattering military defeat and a full-scale assault on its religious identity and institutions? A closer look at the material surrounding this prophecy reveals that these are the words of a man who had counseled surrender to an enemy power and was now advising exiles to "settle down" and work for the welfare of the government that had captured them!

Or consider the word of Job's pious friends. Taken in isolation, Bildad's assertion that Yahweh is always just sounds reassuring: "Does God pervert justice? Or does the Almighty pervert the right?" (Job 8:3). Thus it is a bit of a shock to discover that, within the larger context of the book of Job, these words are seen to be hollow and ineffective; in no way are they a reflection of God's intention in allowing Satan to afflict. Likewise, the story of Philip and the Ethiopian eunuch is sandwiched between an account of Philip's startling successes with the Samaritans (a people roundly despised by the Jews for their syncretistic worship and racially mixed backgrounds) and the conversion of Saul of Tarsus, who was called by the risen Lord to undertake a mission to the "unclean" Gentiles. The placement of a story about a convert who would have been considered unfit for temple worship because he had been physically mutilated between accounts of missions to Samaritans and Gentiles presents us with a perspective that might have eluded us otherwise—that of the infant church expanding with tremendous urgency at the very fringes of society. Pagans, Samaritans, the racially mixed, and the sexually marginal—all those who were excluded from the original covenant because of birth or circumstance—are now welcomed into the new.

The question always arises, *How much* of the surrounding material needs to be read? A general rule of thumb is to let the length of the passage under consideration be one's guide. A short passage usually (but not always) requires less contextual analysis than a longer one. For example, one would normally expect to read about one chapter's worth of material, or slightly more, when dealing with a relatively brief passage (i.e., three to ten verses). If an entire chapter is the subject of consideration, one or more chapters preceding and following it should be perused. (Note: this task is greatly simplified by the use of a study Bible that uses topical subtitles, e.g., the Jerusalem Bible, the New English Bible, or Phillips Modern English New Testament.)

C. *The Canonical Context:* Already we can see new possibilities in these passages as a result of the simplest effort to "place" them in a broader literary context. But the possibilities are greater still when we look at the passage against the backdrop of the full range of material in both testaments (i.e., the "canon"). This is not as immense a task as it might seem, and a good study Bible will have carefully selected passages cross-referenced in the marginal notes. The first step is to examine these cross-references. When we do so we find, for example, that Jeremiah was not alone in his dream of a covenant written on the heart—that Ezekiel and Hosea reached similar conclusions about the ultimate failure of the original covenant, written on stone (see, e.g., Ezek. 11:19-20 and Hos. 2:16-23). We learn too how the early church interpreted these words of Jeremiah when we see them quoted in the book of Hebrews (Heb. 8:6-12; 10:15-18). Here the promise of Christ is seen as a clear warrant for declaring the old covenant "obsolete." In the absence of cross-references in a study Bible, the same citations can be located by looking up references to key words (e.g., "heart" or "covenant, new") in a complete concordance.

Marginal notes and/or a corcordance will help us locate the passage from Isaiah that the Ethiopian eunuch was reading on his way home from Jerusalem. With the help of a concordance we can locate other places in the New Testament where the same Old Testament material is cited in various contexts. By looking up "Ethiopia" in the concordance we get a better sense of what Israel's expectations were concerning this nation: "Because of thy temple at Jerusalem / kings bear gifts to thee. . . . Let bronze be brought from Egypt / Let Ethiopia stretch out her hands to God" (Ps. 68:29-31). A helpful cross-reference in one Bible directs the student to Leviticus 21:16-23—a passage that explains why a eunuch (among others) would have been barred from offering sacrifices in a priestly capacity.

A study of the canonical context does more than simply supply more information. It gives us a sense of how certain themes and ideas changed and developed over time, as well as a heightened appreciation for the interrelatedness of scripture. The more we work with the canonical context of a passage, the more sensitive we become to subtle shades of meaning that would otherwise totally escape our notice.

D. *The Historical Context:* Finally, we need to examine whatever information is available to us about the historical context of the passage being studied—its authorship, dating, and place of origin. Commentaries and Bible dictionary entries on the biblical books and their authors will supply this information, and it is of more than passing interest. Identifying the author and the peculiar circumstances confronting the author's community will often radically affect our interpretation of the passage.

It is not enough to see Jeremiah simply as an "Old Testament prophet"; we need to know that Jeremiah preached before, during, and after the fall of Jerusalem to Nebuchadnezzar (in 598 B.C.)—and that he preached "treason" or submission rather than resistance to enemy occupation. It does not require too much reflection to reach the conclusion that such a stand would result in terrible personal pain and suffering, and it is against this background of personal (as well as national) defeat that Jeremiah 31:31-34 needs to be read and interpreted.

Similarly, if we are studying the Acts passage it will make a difference to our analysis if we are aware that the account of Philip and the Ethiopian eunuch was almost certainly written by a Gentile who had a profound interest not only in the expansion of the church universal but in the spiritual destinies of marginal people. Clearly, this type of information greatly enhances our understanding and appreciation of the story's significance.

Verse-by-Verse Analysis: Does It Mean What It Says?

Traditionally, the study of scripture has been characterized by thorough and precise attention to detail. Its immense value and antiquity have prompted scholars to labor away their lives on relatively small portions of material—a specter that is daunting to even the most earnest of students. For a generation accustomed to "instant gratification" in many departments of life the prospect of a relatively slow and painstaking verse-by-verse analysis of scripture is sufficient justification for relegating serious theological work to the "theologians." It is not enough to say, "Try it, you'll like it!"—the task seems overwhelming.

Fortunately this resistance to precision work can be overcome if one is willing to work with patience and manageable amounts of material. Basically, there are three concepts that need to be communicated to the beginning Bible student:

1. *The work can be shared.* In group study each person can be held responsible for a small portion of the material—perhaps for as little as a single verse, depending upon the length of the passage studied and the size of the group.

2. *The rewards of serious study are cumulative and directly proportional to the effort expended.* One quickly discovers that even a little bit of additional research can make a substantial contribution to a clearer understanding of a text. Further, it is not necessary to repeat the same operations every time one encounters the same key word in subsequent passages. Serious study not only provides short-term illumination, it is also a long-term investment!

3. *Students can learn to be increasingly selective and efficient in the process of research.* Increasing familiarity with biblical material and the research process itself will help students focus their efforts more efficiently. The process outlined here represents the *maximum* possibilities for exploring a passage; it does not need to be followed slavishly.

In fact, once students have tried it, they almost always do like it, and the problem becomes that of finding ways for group members to more effectively share during discussion the results of their research (see chapter 7). Once converted to the idea that serious study is not only possible but immensely valuable, the student still faces a serious internal barrier to greater understanding of the text, however. *The single greatest obstacle to understanding scripture is the sincere conviction on the part of the reader that he or she already knows what the text means simply because it sounds so familiar.* The realization that the "familiar" remains the unknown and that the comforting dimension of scripture must often become the confronting comes only through the experience of actually wrestling with biblical texts. To begin with, the student must proceed on "faith."

A. *Identifying Key Words:* The primary tools for verse-by-verse analysis are a good Bible dictionary, a theological wordbook, and a complete concordance.[1] The general rule to follow is that every "key word" (i.e., proper names, place names, references to historical events, religious customs and institutions, theological terms, etc.) should be investigated either by reading the appropriate entry in the Bible dictionary and wordbook and/or by referring to related material in the concordance. Table III shows the key words in the two passages we have already discussed *italicized.*

TABLE III

Identifying Key Words

Jeremiah 31:31-34 (RSV)	Acts 8:26-39 (RSV)
Behold, the days are coming, says the *LORD*, when I will make *a new covenant* with the *house of Israel* and the *house of Judah,* not like the covenant which I made with their *fathers* when I took them out of the land of *Egypt,* my covenant which they *broke,* though I was their *husband,* says the LORD. But this is the covenant which I will make with the house of Israel after those days, says the LORD: I will put *my law* within them, and I will write it upon their *hearts;* and *I will be their God,* and they shall be *my people.* And no longer shall each man *teach* his *neighbor* and each his *brother,* saying, "*Know* the LORD," for they shall all know me from the least of them to the greatest; for I will *forgive* their *iniquity,* and I will *remember* their *sin* no more.	But an *angel* of the *Lord* said to *Philip,* "Rise and go toward the south to the road that goes down from *Jerusalem* to *Gaza.*" This is a desert road. And he rose and went. And behold, an *Ethiopian,* a *eunuch,* minister of the *Candace,* queen of the Ethiopians, in charge of all her treasure, had come to Jerusalem to *worship* and was returning; seated in his chariot, he was reading the *prophet Isaiah.* And the *Spirit* said to Philip, "Go up and join this chariot." So Philip ran to him, and heard him reading Isaiah the prophet, and asked, "Do you *understand* what you are reading? And he said, "How can I, unless some one *guides* me?" And he invited Philip to come up and sit with him. Now the passage of the *scripture* which he was reading was this: "As a *sheep* led to the *slaughter* or a *lamb* before its shearer is dumb, so he *opens not his mouth.* In his *humiliation justice* was denied him. Who can describe his *generation?* For his *life* is taken up from the earth." And the eunuch said to Philip, "About whom, pray, does the prophet say this, about himself or about some one else?" Then

> Philip opened his mouth, and beginning with this scripture he told him the *good news* of *Jesus*. And as they went along the road they came to some *water*, and the eunuch said, "See, here is water! What is to prevent my being *baptized*?" And he commanded the chariot to stop, and they both went down into the water, Philip and the eunuch, and he baptized him. And when they came up out of the water, the Spirit of the Lord caught up Philip; and the eunuch saw him no more, and went on his way rejoicing.

A student working on the Jeremiah passage, for example, will find dictionary entries for most of the underlined words, with the possible exception of "husband" and "know," which happen to be found in Richardson's *Theological Wordbook*. Is it necessary, then, to read every word of each entry? No. If the work is being shared by more than one person the student would concencentrate on those entries corresponding to the key words in the assigned verses. For example, the person responsible for verse 31 would study the entries on "covenant," "Israel, house of," and "Judah, house of." In the process of studying, the student would learn something about the origin and development of Israel's covenantal relationship with her God as well as the division of Yahweh's chosen people into two separate, hostile kingdoms—both of which figure in Jeremiah's message of hope and salvation.

The student responsible for verse 32 would also study the entry on "covenant" as well as that on "Egypt," which will describe the historical circumstances that led up to the giving of the original covenant on Mount Sinai and thus underscore the significance of an arrangement Jeremiah is claiming is no longer valid. The image of Yahweh as "husband" should be explored with the concordance: Does this image of Yahweh appear elsewhere in either the Old or New Testaments? Is it confined to Jeremiah, or do other prophets make use of it? How does this image color our concept of the covenantal relationship?

Verse 33 introduces three important new words: "law," "heart," and "people, my." The Bible dictionary entry on "law" will be lengthy and does not have to be read in full, but it is essential to understand the relationship of "law" to "covenant" in order to make sense of this passage, and one may read selectively with this question in mind. The term "heart" provides us with a classic example of the type of word the beginning student is likely to overlook because he or she is "sure" of its meaning. In fact, the entry on heart will reveal that in biblical times it was the human heart (and not the brain) which was seen to be the seat of intelligence, moral sensitivity, and "will"—an insight that will radically affect our understanding of the passage! Similarly, the term "people" may appear self-explanatory, but when Israel referred to herself as Yahweh's "people" she had something very definite in mind. An exploration of this term using a concordance will lead the student directly into the foundational concept of "election"—a notion that the events of Jeremiah's day called into question. How might such an exploration proceed?

First, the enormous number of references to "people" cited in the concordance precludes an exhaustive study of the term. *Cruden's Complete Concordance* uses helpful subdivisions with terms that appear frequently in scripture, so in this case, it is possible to easily locate references to "my people." Even so, the list we are left to work with is extremely long, so it is necessary to pose specific questions before examining the references. For example, we might ask which books appear to have the largest number of references to "my people." Interestingly, the "winners" in this category are Isaiah, Jeremiah, and Ezekiel. Jeremiah and Ezekiel were contemporaries who shared in the catastrophic events leading up to and following the fall of Jerusalem. Furthermore, almost two-thirds of the references in Isaiah date from the same general period (or slightly later). What does this suggest about the impact of a crushing military defeat and consequent exile on Israel's sense of her own "chosenness"? Limiting our study just to additional references in Jeremiah, what can be said about Yahweh's expectations for his "people" and their ability to fulfill them?

Finally, verse 34 requires us to learn more about "sin" and "forgiveness," especially as these were understood in the Old

Testament. The dictionary entries for these terms will make this historical distinction and illumine the direct and essential link between the concepts of "sin" and "covenant." A glance at the concordance will give us some clues as to whether or not the term "forgive/forgiveness" is used frequently by any of the prophets. (It is not!) Verbs such as "teach" and "know" are also surprisingly important to understanding Jeremiah's concerns, especially in light of what we have already learned about the meaning of "heart." Both verbs may be fruitfully explored with the aid of a concordance. Again, most helpfully, *Cruden's Complete Concordance* has listed together all those references which speak of "knowing that [Yahweh is] the Lord," and the incidence of this phrase in the books of Exodus and the exilic prophet Ezekiel turns out to be striking.

B. *Using the Study Selection Principle:* It is important to stress that the reading of Bible dictionary and wordbook entries for key words needs to be done *selectively*. For one reason, there is seldom enough time for a single individual to research all the key words thoroughly. Second, the beginning student who is confronted with a large amount of new (and often fascinating) information is easily sidetracked by some entrancing bit of data which has no real bearing on the passage being studied. Although some such "excursions" are inevitable and often pique the student's curiosity, time limitations make it essential that one develop a reliable sense of what is relevant *in terms of the congregational context* for study. It is during verse-by-verse analysis that one is most likely to lose sight of the group's immediate agenda (see A above, under "Context Questions") and the governing principle this ought to provide. This means not *every* key word need be investigated in any given situation; and it also means that one must sometimes read only those portions of an entry which are relevant to the congregational context. Therefore the student needs to pause occasionally in the heat of research and ask herself, "Why am I doing this?" and "Which of these leads should I take time to pursue?" This kind of selectivity takes time to develop, but the ultimate goal should always be *to locate and take note of that information which throws new light on the theological significance of the passage.*

C. *Identifying Theological Themes and Issues:* Generally speaking, people undertake the study of scripture not because they are interested in ancient civilizations or the history of religion but simply because they are deeply in earnest about trying to discern God's will for their own lives and the life of their church community. Unfortunately, the typical church member tends to make a false distinction between what he or she considers to be the "historical" and the "spiritual" dimensions of scripture. The former may be interesting to some—usually specialists—but it is the latter, the so-called spiritual meaning of the Bible, which they believe is truly important for the church today.

The practiced student of scripture has learned that biblical religion never makes this sharp distinction between the historical and the spiritual, the timebound and the timeless. In both the Old and New Testaments God is seen as revealing himself *through* historical events—not outside of them. It is scandalous but true that it is in the erratic history of a particular (and very peculiar) people that the Western world has grounded its spiritual identity. In what sense can we say, then, that this particular reality should be determinative of the way in which the church deals with its scriptures today?

The research process described thus far takes full account of this scandalous particularity. The slow, sometimes painstaking work with reference tools is never undertaken simply for the sake of more information, helpful though this might be. *It is undertaken because it is essential to discovering the theological significance of biblical texts, and it is precisely this dimension of the texts which makes them of interest and value to the church today.*

Although, for the sake of clarity, we are treating the identification of theological issues as a separate category, the process of identification does not occur in isolation from actual research. *It is in the study of particulars that questions and issues of general interest emerge.* Strangely enough, the "firstfruits" of the research process are not answers but *more questions,* and these questions are, quite literally, the "offering" we bring to our fellow students.

In our study of Jeremiah 31:31-34 the additional reading done on terms such as "covenant," "heart," "law," and "sin" presents us with a series of questions for which there are no simple answers: Were the terms of the covenant made on Sinai really impossible for human beings to fulfill? If so, why would

Yahweh initiate a relationship that was fated to fail? In what sense could the terms of the Sinai covenant ever be said to be "written on the heart"? Would such a transformation be totally miraculous? Does it make sense to continue talking of sin and obedience in the context of Jeremiah's vision of the Torah-inscribed heart? Does Jeremiah's vision correspond to the New Covenant initiated by Jesus the Christ?

Questions of this sort cannot be classified as either "historical" or "spiritual." They are, quite simply, the "gut-level" issues with which Israel struggled at various points in her history, and, properly interpreted, they are of vital importance to the church today. Disciplined study brings us face to face with profound theological problems and—further—provides us with something beyond mere opinion with which to tackle them.

Applications: What Difference Does It Make?

A. *The Final "Interpretive" Paraphrase:* Bible study is never truly completed until we have attempted to reflect in a careful, systematic way upon what we have learned, and in reflecting, make creative and responsible applications to the situation of the church today. Generally speaking, the most effective way to marshal one's thoughts is to put them in writing, and so the research process is concluded (as it was begun) with a paraphrase though, at this point, we are equipped to expand our statement with considerable interpretive material.

To review, let us consider a typical initial reaction to the popular and overly familiar Jeremiah passage. One reason Jeremiah's prophecy about the "new covenant" written on the heart is popular is because it seems to emphasize the failure of the "old," Sinaitic covenant and thus point toward the revelation of God in Jesus Christ. The Law, which commonly has negative, harsh connotations for Christians (especially Protestants), is overshadowed here by the affective image of the heart—a soft, palpable, "living" reality—associated in modern minds with emotions, motivation, the "inner person," and so on. Yet a careful study of this passage, or even just a more careful *reading* of it, shows that this rather sentimental interpretation is totally inadequate.

God's promise of a new covenant is not, in Jeremiah's eyes, a simple rejection of the old. Our study of the passage will have provided us with some basic information about the historical circumstances leading up to the giving of the covenant on Mount Sinai—circumstances that included experiences of slavery, the threat of impending disaster, and dramatic deliverance. In addition we shall have learned, if we didn't know already, that the *content* of the covenant was the *Torah,* the "teaching" or "law," which had shaped not only Israel's worship practices but every other aspect of her shared, national existence as well. *Torah* or "Law" was what made Israel "Yahweh's people." Does Jeremiah assert that the day is coming when when *Torah* is to be abandoned? Hardly. Although Jeremiah says the new covenant is "not like" the covenant Yahweh made with Israel's ancestors, the difference does not extend to changing the *content* of the covenant, for what is to be written on the heart is still *Torah.* Nothing is said to lessen the significance of Law in the life of Israel. In fact, the import of this passage is to make the Law more vitally important than ever. Since Israel has proved herself totally unable to obey a covenant written on stone, it is necessary for Yahweh to inscribe the Law on the heart of each person. In this way the fulfillment of *Torah* will no longer depend on the whims of a weak and faithless people.

What is "new," then, is not the *content* of revelation but the *manner* in which revelation is received and lived out. *What is to be changed, transformed, or created anew is the person, not the Law.* The Law written on the heart becomes more powerful than ever. Instead of being an external, confronting force, it becomes an internal, compelling force—a primal instinct and not a set of precepts that must be taught to each new generation.

And what does Jeremiah say is the purpose of this transformation of human nature? The prophet claims that this change will ensure universal knowledge of Yahweh and acknowledgment of his lordship. This instinctual "knowing" or total experiencing of Yahweh is what makes Israel "his people." Chosenness is no longer dependent on obedience, for the transformation of the heart means, as we have seen, the

138

transformation of *intellect* and *will*. Israel is to have no will separate from Yahweh's. The knowledge of good and evil—in short, the sin—which came as the fruit of disobedience will have lost all power to separate Israel from her God.

B. *Identifying Yourself and Your Congregation in the Passage:* What Jeremiah has to say to the church today will, of course, to some extent be determined by the particular circumstances of individual congregations. What was originally meant as a message of hope and consolation is still just that, but Jeremiah's emphasis on the absolute integrity of the Law contains a cautionary note, especially for those church communities which consistently emphasize what they like to call "religion of the heart." It is all too easy to affirm Jeremiah's claim that we need a covenant written on the heart *while ignoring just what it is he expects to find written on the heart!* Moreover, "religion of the heart" in Jeremiah's sense includes the totality of the person—the intellect and the will as well as the emotions.

The clear message of hope that infuses this passage and that holds for the church in every age is Yahweh's determination not to abandon his people even (and especially) in times of crisis. If the covenant—that which makes them his—cannot be transmitted and maintained in one form, then the manner of its maintainance and transmission must be changed, and changed in such a way that the identity of God's elect is forever assured. Nothing—not even sin of the gravest sort—can affect Yahweh's determination in this respect. Our study of Jeremiah should do more than console us. It should prompt us to struggle for a deeper understanding of just what it is God intends to write on our hearts—to know from the very center of our being the basis of our identity, what it means to be "his people."

C. *Responding Through Change:* It is not enough in our search for meaning and understanding simply to intellectually "apply" the message of the text to the situation of the local congregation. Our direct encounter with biblical texts is in the nature of a personal, convenantal relationship with scripture itself. Israel knew that to "hear" the word of God was also to "do" it. Exegesis must therefore always be an invitation to action. If we fail to respond faithfully to the Word we have heard, we undermine that very relationship which the church claims it exists to nurture; and although Jeremiah assures us that God is determined to maintain that relationship no matter what, we cannot refuse the risk of change without hardening our hearts to the point where *nothing* can be written on them.

(N.B. An abbreviated form of the exegetical process suitable for regular use is to be found in Appendix D.)

CHAPTER SEVEN

The Community Responds:

Techniques for Fruitful and Disciplined Discussion

A lawyer stood up to put him to the test, saying, "Teacher, what shall I do to inherit eternal life?" He said to him, "What is written in the law? How do you read?"   Luke 10:25-26

Through the process of exegesis the faith community "listens" to the Word of God. But in a relationship of active dialogue it is necessary for the community to do more than simply "listen." It must also respond to what it has heard. So it is that the fruits of exegetical study are not fully *digested* until they have been shared with others.

The sharing of insights and information through group discussion accomplishes at least two things: first, it challenges us to report truthfully what we have "heard," i.e., it tests the objectivity of our study/"listening" skills; and second, it provides an appropriate forum for a *collective* (and not simply a personal) response to God's Word. This vital form of exchange between the church and its scriptures requires discussion leaders who are not only familiar with the exegetical study process; they must have additional skills as well: sensitivity to persons and issues, a good sense of timing, confidence, and flexibility. Yet with strong motivation and opportunities for practice, these skills can be developed and refined. The steps outlined below are fundamental to bringing the study process to a satisfying conclusion in group discussion:

Thorough Preparation

Although everyone in the group will be involved in researching the text, the leader has a special responsibility to be well informed. Her approach to studying the text will be much the same as that of the other participants, but she will need to pay special attention to identifying the *theological themes and issues* (see also pp. 135-37 and 176-78). Whereas group members may be doing intensive, verse-by-verse exegesis, the leader must be concerned with the passage as a totality, especially as it relates to material the group has studied previously or may study soon in the future. The purpose of the leader's research is *not* to prepare her to answer every possible question that might arise but to help her anticipate what those questions might be and to make an intelligent selection about which questions to pursue in the actual discussion.

Context Considerations

A careful examination of the text in its immediate and historical contexts should suggest several points of departure, yet only a few (maybe only one) can be dealt with effectively in the time allotted for discussion. Which criteria should be applied in selecting questions?

The primary consideration should always be the *congregational context* in which the passage is being studied. Is the text one of a series of biblical passages comprising a Lenten study on the sacraments? Is your adult education class studying the Gospel of Mark as an example of the way the early church did theology? Perhaps you are planning a single-session workshop on evangelism for the membership committee. In each case, the specific needs of the local congregation, study group, or committee should be determinative of the central focus of the discussion. Although the same text could be used in all of the above situations, the types of questions addressed to it would be different according to the immediate context.

Let us, for example, look at all the possibilities for discussion within a single, very familiar text: Mark's account of the baptism of Jesus (1:1-11). Depending upon your objectives, this text could be used as the basis for a discussion of the sacrament of baptism, the relationship of Jesus to John the Baptist and other prophetic figures, the way in which the early church used the Hebrew scriptures to interpret Jesus' identity and ministry, the meaning of "repentance" in the context of conversion experiences, empowerment by the Holy Spirit, and so on. It is essential for the leader to realize and accept the fact that there is always more gold in a text than can be mined in a single research effort or discussion. Therefore, *select only those questions or issues which draw attention to your overall objectives as they are shaped by the immediate context of the study.*

Identifying Basic Theological Questions

The best discussion questions are always questions of interpretation—questions to which there are no easy yes or no answers, no pat responses.[1] Scripture is always a rich resource for discussion simply because it does require a great deal of "interpretation." Theological issues, i.e., questions involving our relationship to God and God's relationship to us, are always open to further interpretation and debate; and at the same time, these are issues to which the church must constantly address itself. These are the issues that determine *what* we believe and *how* we will live.

Basic theological issues and questions are imbedded in the texts themselves. Sometimes they leap out at us; in other cases they surface only as the result of long and careful scrutiny of textual details that would at first appear irrelevant. For the sake of illustration let us suppose you plan to use Mark 1:1-11 as one of a series of texts relating to the sacraments of the church. There are any number of passages relating to baptism, but this one is unique in at least one respect: it describes the baptism of Jesus himself, whom the church labels "sinless." A question that leaps out at us is, Why did Jesus seek baptism from his cousin John? This is a good example of a theological or "interpretive" question. There is no clear explanation in the text which can supply a "factual" answer. Furthermore, it raises an issue about which many people will feel genuine doubt and curiosity—two very necessary ingredients for a lively discussion.

Yet before we can answer this question directly we must address ourselves to a whole host of questions *suggested by* the initial question: What do we know about the background and beliefs of both Jesus and John? Do other Gospel accounts supply more information? How do their treatments of the relationship between Jesus and John compare to that of Mark's? What, if anything, is Jesus reported to have said about John and his baptism? What kinds of experiences might we assume that Jesus and John had in common? How did the content of their preaching differ? What distinguishes John's baptism from previous practices? From the baptism practiced by Jesus' disciples? Would Jesus have felt the need to "repent"? What motivated the other persons coming to John for baptism? The list of possible follow-up questions to the basic theological question (Why did Jesus seek baptism from John?) is practically endless.

Suppose, however, you wished to use the same text as part of a study on how the early church made use of the Hebrew scriptures in its theologizing about Jesus. If we assume that the church would continue to value and consult these scriptures in the first place, the first question that presents itself is this: Which portions of Scripture would they have been likely to use and why? After establishing which portions of scripture are either quoted or alluded to in this passage (there are two direct quotations: Isa. 40:3 and Ps. 2:7), the group would need to examine these citations in their original settings: Who wrote the Isaiah text and when? What particular historical circumstances confronted the faith community at the time these words were written? What do the terms "messenger" and "wilderness" refer to? Does this quotation appear elsewhere in the New Testament? Does the situation of the faith community addressed by Mark correspond in any way to what Israel was experiencing when the Isaiah passage was written? What is the setting of the quotation from Psalm 2? On what sort of occasions does it appear to have been used? Would it have been used in the same way when Jesus was alive? How might it have been interpreted at the time Mark was writing? How might

144

either one or both of these passages have shaped Israel's expectations concerning the long-awaited Messiah? When lifted out of their original settings and placed in the account of Jesus' baptism does their meaning change?

Whichever basic theological question you choose, it is obvious that either one will generate ample material for a full discussion of anywhere from thirty minutes to two hours! This is a cause not for despair, however, but for rejoicing, for *the true test of a good discussion question is the number of follow-up questions it generates*. What is more, the opportunity to explore a single, interesting issue in some depth provides more real learning and generates more curiosity than a scattershot approach that attempts to cover *all* the important issues in a passage during a solitary sitting.

To summarize, the leader's preparation should focus on identifying the theological issues raised in the passage, framing carefully worded questions on those which relate most directly to the immediate needs and study focus of the group with which she will be working. Generally speaking, two or three basic theological questions with accompanying follow-up questions will provide more than enough fuel for the average discussion. A good basic question will require at least thirty minutes of discussion time.

Learning Which Questions Not to Ask

Once people discover how exhilarating and illuminating the study process itself can be, they are tempted to make that process itself the focus of discussion. Usually this is a mistake, unless, of course you are specifically trying to analyze the process and its impact on the individual. Solid research is the foundation of a good discussion, but research or study questions—e.g., What is the literary context of this passage?—are not good discussion questions!

The study process is geared to sifting through a relatively large amount of information, most of it historical or linguistic in nature. The goal of this process is not to amass as much knowledge about the Bible as possible (worthy though this goal may be!); rather, it is to locate that information which *throws new light on the theological significance of the passage under consideration.* For this reason it is relatively redundant and not very interesting to use questions that appear on the study instructions *as discussion questions.* The relevant information unearthed during study is likely to emerge in a much more germane fashion in responses to follow-up questions. Historical data are most appropriately used to *substantiate or explain* a particular theological interpretation rather than simply for their own sake.[2]

Again, let us look at an example. Were we to study Mark 1:1-11 in a sacramental context, one of the follow-up questions used might be this:

Leader: Bill, do you think John was the originator of the practice of baptism?

Bill: No, probably not. According to my Bible dictionary, baptismal rites were practiced just prior to the Christian era.

Leader: Could you explain why this was done?

Bill: Yes, baptism was used to initiate Gentiles who wanted to convert to Judaism. I also learned that priests used to take ritual baths when they had contaminated themselves, so the idea does not appear to have originated with John.

The information Bill shares is very important for an understanding of Mark 1:1-11 and could only be uncovered as a result of some methodical work on his part. Its significance, however, is much clearer in the context of the question, Was John the originator of the practice of baptism? than it would be if the question had been simply, What did you learn about the history of baptism?

Another common mistake discussion leaders make is to pose questions that are too vague, or general enough to apply to almost any passage. The question, Why did Jesus seek baptism from John? will spark more specific and better-supported responses than would the more general question, Why do Christians practice the rite of baptism? The same thing applies, no matter what the congregational context may be. Why would Mark open his Gospel with these words of Isaiah? is more provocative than, Why would Mark begin his Gospel with a quotation from the Old Testament? Vague questions such as,

Why is this an interesting passage? should be avoided; and *never* begin a discussion with the question, What do you *feel* about this passage? This is nothing but an invitation to *eisegesis* or a subjective reading of meaning *into* the passage!

Establishing Ground Rules for Participants

Before beginning work with any group it is essential that certain ground rules be established for productive and satisfying discussion. The following rules have proved extremely effective:

A. *Everyone participates to some extent in the study process.* Insisting that the preparatory work be shared accomplishes at least two purposes: It gives everyone a personal stake in the outcome of the discussion, and it allows for more substantial and informed contributions. In addition it provides the most compelling introduction possible to the research tools, increases one's skill in their use, and invariably whets the appetite for more insight and information. If we fail to encourage joint responsibility for study, we simply continue to encourage a *passive* relationship to scripture in which we are content to let someone else do our thinking for us, and we are left with nothing to share but opinions.

B. *Everyone shares in the discussion.* Each participant should be made to feel that his or her contributions are vital to the health and success of the group. Whether or not a participant discovered anything that contributes to some startling new insight, the very act of sharing contributes to the construction of a *collective* response. Sharing a frustration or a failure to resolve a pressing question can also be valuable to the entire group; and the person who can pinpoint an issue or ask questions that lead to new insights should be invited to lead the discussion next time!

C. *Theological positions must always be offered as "interpretations," not as "facts."* Although historians and archaeologists are constantly making new discoveries, much of what we now "know" about the Bible still remains in the realm of the relatively speculative. Bible scholars can, at best, offer us "informed opinions." Therefore Bible students need to learn to preface their own remarks with such things as "In my view

. . ." or "I would interpret the passage in this way . . ." and *not* "This is what it means!"

D. *Theological positions should be substantiated.* When a participant takes a given position on a theological issue, he or she should be prepared to substantiate that position *on the basis of what is to be found in the actual text under consideration* and in the reference works consulted. Providing evidence for a position will not rule out honest differences of opinion, but taking a position because "that's what I learned in Sunday school" is to put an end to the discussion! Participants should be alerted at the outset that they will be expected to ground their opinions on terms that are open to the scrutiny of the group.

E. *Theological diversity is anticipated, respected, and valued for the richness it provides to the process of study and discussion.* The tradition of scripture study and debate long antedates the Christian church. According to Luke (2:41-51), Jesus himself was initiated into the joys of theological dialogue at the tender age of twelve. The Gospel stories about Jesus' encounters with the scribes and pharisees underscore not only his knowledge of scripture but also his ability to "play the game," so to speak, when issues of interpretation were at stake (see Matt. 22:41-46). Seldom, if ever, has the church spoken with a single voice on *any* issue.

Internalizing these ground rules for participants will not take long if the leader exemplifies them herself by setting a tone that combines scrupulous attention to the text with a genuine appreciation of theological diversity.

Conducting the Discussion

A successful discussion begins with a challenging question that poses a real issue for participants. In most cases this will be a theological or interpretive question. In order to answer the question, a series of carefully chosen and well-sequenced follow-up questions *prepared in advance* should be used to guide the discussion so that a satisfactory resolution is finally reached.

A. *Constructing Good Follow-Up Questions:* A simple and effective strategy for structuring a discussion is to make up a list of follow-up questions that reflect the actual sequence of material in the text. In addition, your follow-up questions should assume a knowledge of the literary context and possibly some exploration of the canonical context as well, depending on the expertise and previous experiences of the group one is working with.

For the sake of illustration let us suppose that an experienced group of Bible students is studying John 13:31-35 as one of a series of texts on the subject of "commandments." The leader has decided that, given the congregational context, the most fruitful interpretive question is, Is there really anything *new* about Jesus' "new commandment" to his disciples? Listed below are the follow-up questions prepared for this single issue, with the expectation that close to an hour would be spent in discussing this single issue. Note that they first establish the *setting* of these remarks with questions about the literary context:

Basic interpretive question:

Is there anything really "new" about Jesus' "new commandment"?

Follow-up questions:

1. At what point in time does Jesus give this new commandment? (literary context)

2. What does the author of John consider worth reporting about Jesus' last evening with his disciples? (literary context)

3. Does the text tell us *why* Jesus washes his disciples' feet? (literary context)

4. Who usually washes the guests' feet? Then what would one infer from Jesus' act? (literary context)

5. What else gets reported about this last evening together? (literary context)

6. What does Jesus say after Judas gets up and leaves? (vv. 31-32)

7. What does Jesus mean when he says he has been "glorified"?

8. What does the word "glorify" mean? (vv. 31-32) Did anyone do a word study on "glorify"? Did anyone consult a dictionary or wordbook? What did you discover? (vv. 31-32)

9. Is Jesus abandoning his disciples when he tells them that they cannot follow him? (v. 33)

10. What is the content of the "new commandment"?

11. Does Jesus suggest that his love for his disciples is different from the way anyone else would love them? If so, how? (v. 34)

12. Is there anything else in the Gospel of John about "commandments"? What do these references say? (literary/canonical context)

13. Would someone volunteer to paraphrase or restate the "new commandment"? (an "almost final" paraphrase used as a summarizing device)

14. Do we agree that this is an accurate paraphrase?

15. What does Jesus say are the consequences of obeying the "new commandment"? (v. 35)

16. Let's go back now to our original question: Is there anything really "new" about Jesus' "new commandment"? (basic interpretive question)

17. Is this a commandment *you* could obey? Why? Why not? (applications)

B. *Following Through on Responses to Questions: Although the leader's prior work on follow-up questions will generally determine the direction* the discussion will take, it will not necessarily (nor should it) *control* the discussion. Well-prepared students will have plenty of their own questions to ask and probably will not hesitate to ask them. Often the responses a leader gets will suggest further questions that need to be pursued. The leader must be flexible enough to recognize and anticipate these unanticipated questions which are "hidden" in a previous response.

To return to an earlier example, let us suppose you are leading a discussion on Mark 1:1-11, and you pose the following question:

Leader: Anna, what do you think is meant by the term "John's baptism"?

Anna: Well, Mark states that John baptized with water and that his baptism was a baptism of "repentance."

Does Anna's response answer the question sufficiently to warrant proceeding to the next follow-up question? No. There are several more questions hidden in Anna's answer. For example, What does Mark mean by "repentance"? Is Mark suggesting that there can be baptisms without water? Was John's understanding of baptism as a symbol of repentance an innovation? Since Mark, to be precise, refers to John's baptism as a baptism of "repentance for the forgiveness of sins," we are confronted with even more possibilities to pursue. Depending on the congregational context of the study, the leader may or may not decide to pursue definitions of terms such as "forgiveness" and "sins" as far as she has already pursued, say, "repentance." The point to be made here is this: *Leaders are too often tempted to drop a fruitful line of questioning before its possibilities have been exhausted.* More persistant questioning of this kind often reveals that participants are operating with different definitions of key terms, with each one assuming that *his* meaning is the self-evident one and commonly held by everyone. Theological terms always need definition and clarification, so *take time to do this,* resorting to reference books on the spot, if necessary.

C. *Leader, Teacher, or Missionary?* Another temptation facing participants and leaders alike is the expectation that the leader is a resource who can be counted on to supply information and answers. Often the leader does have a better background in scripture than other members of the group, but when she begins to answer questions put to her she crosses the line that separates "leader" from "teacher," and immediately the stakes are lowered for the participants. Ideally, the leader should answer every question put to her with another question: Does anyone else have a response to that? What does it say in the text? Which reference tool would you consult to find that information? Occasionally time and circumstances absolutely require a substantive response from the leader, but these should be kept to a minimum. One way to eliminate much of this temptation is for the leader to select only those issues for discussion which present real issues and problems for her personally.

While some leaders are tempted to become "teachers," others cannot resist the urge to preach and convert. Unfortunately, nothing is more fatal to effective dialogue with scripture than a heavy-handed attempt on the part of a convinced Christian to use a forum for group reflection and discourse as a "pulpit." To provide a forum for dialogue it is necessary to *trust* in the power of God's Word *to speak for itself and do its own converting.* (In fact, surprisingly few people *do* trust the scriptures to this extent!) That leader is most effective who, instead of interposing herself between the reader and the biblical texts, acts to remove all such "obstacles" to enlightenment. (For a more extended discussion of the subject of "conversion," see chapter 8.)

D. *Pacing the Discussion:* Pacing the discussion is central to its success. A flagging discussion can be revived by a good follow-up question directed to a specific individual: "Irma, did you find any additional references to John's baptism in the other three Gospels?" (Directing questions to individuals further ensures wider group participation and makes it more difficult for one person to monopolize the discussion.) The issue of timing, generally speaking, requires more skill than any other aspect of discussion leadership. There is never enough time when a good discussion is underway, and careful planning does not always ensure that a discussion will proceed "on schedule." Allowing approximately thirty minutes for each basic theological question and follow-up questions is a good rule of thumb, but what happens when you have only forty-five minutes allotted for discussion and at least three absolutely vital theological issues to pursue?

It is important to restate here that *it is preferable to do justice to one issue rather than to slight several.* During a single forty-five-minute session it is possible to do a solid job with one basic theological question and still allow time for some evaluative questions—questions that relate to the "Applications" section of the study instructions (p. 137).

E. *Ending the Discussion: The Problem of Applying What Has Been Learned:* Most of the allotted discussion time will be spent examining the text itself, in its own terms; yet the dialogue with scripture is never really complete until some attempt has been made to reflect on and respond to what the passage has to say to the church today. Questions of application are evaluative (rather than interpretive) in nature. They should never be used to begin a discussion, but they are almost always the most appropriate way of ending one. Deciding when and how to move from interpretation to evaluation is difficult but very important. It would not be wise, for example, having covered two basic questions, to move into a third if you have to end the discussion in fifteen minutes. In some instances, it may be germane to the discussion to include a question of application before having exhausted a basic theological question, but care must be taken to make sure that the discussion is not then diverted into an entirely different direction: "The trouble with my pastor is . . ." or, "The same thing happened last year in our church . . ." While this type of anecdotal material may be valuable in illustrating a point, too much of it can transform a discussion into a gossip session. The evaluation process is always most valuable when it remains issue-oriented: "Does the rite of baptism practiced by the church today bear any resemblance to John's baptism" or "Is the church still using the Old Testament as creatively in its teaching and preaching as the church of Mark's time was able to do?

A Summary of Do's and Don'ts for Discussion Leaders

Remember, discussion-leading is an *art,* not a science. It takes sensitivity to others, a good sense of timing, imagination, and flexibility. Nothing will help you more to acquire the necessary skills than actual practice; but in the process of learning, there are several important things to keep in mind. If you keep in mind that your primary role as leader or facilitator is to *empower other people,* your efforts will surely meet with some measure of success!

DO:	DON'T:
Try to direct questions back to other members of the group. What ideas do *they* have? Where would they look for answers?	Become an authoritative "answer person" for the group.
Keep drawing people's attention back to the biblical text. What precisely does it *say* or *not say?*	Deliver a lecture on the results of your own research before anyone else has had a chance to share.
Be prepared to explain *how* you researched the passage. It is usually more effective to share skills and not just information.	Spend so much time discussing background information that you never get around to considering the relevance of the passage for the local church community.
Keep time limitations in mind. Be flexible without disregarding the need for some structure.	Allow one person to monopolize the discussion, including (and especially) yourself.
Limit discussion on background information to those data which really do throw light on the theological issue raised by the passage. (This means you have to know what the issue is!)	Present your own theological position on the passage as if it were *the correct* interpretation, instead of being, simply, *your* interpretation.
Keep nurturing the idea within the group that *everyone* has something valuable and unique to contribute to both the study and discussion process.	Get bogged down on the issue of whether the passage is "literally" true or not. (Acknowledge that there will always be significant differences of opinion here.)

CHAPTER EIGHT

The Spirit Has the Last Word:

The Conversion of the Exegete

Truly, I say to you, unless you turn and become like children, you will never enter the kingdom of heaven.   Matthew 18:3

Two Important Parables and How We Misread Them

The noted New Testament scholar Krister Stendahl tells of hearing a sermon preached in his local church on the provocative parable of the laborers in the vineyard (Matt. 20:1-16). This disturbing little story about an employer who is willing to pay the same wage to everyone, regardless of the amount of time and effort expended, is not exactly a favorite of the person in the pew! Accustomed as we are to believing in the virtues of early rising and hard work, we may find the absence of simple justice in this parable offensive. Observing this to be the case, Professor Stendahl recalls that the pastor first gave "the usual boy scout message": "The Boy Scout does his duty without consideration of reward. . . . [and furthermore] one should not really think about different rates of reward because the one and only true reward is Jesus Christ." But this Lutheran pastor, claims Stendahl, was a good preacher who read his Bible. Paraphrasing the conclusion of the sermon, Stendahl writes:

> But of course that is actually *not* what the text is about. Do you know who the eleventh hour folks are? They are we, the Gentiles. It was

155

Israel who worked through the whole long heat of sacred history and we lazy Gentiles came in at the last moment and got the same pay.[1]

Whenever I tell this story to students I always get the same surprised response. Invariably, faithful church members and conscientious committee workers find this parable difficult and distasteful because they automatically (and perhaps unconsciously) identify themselves with the long-toiling early risers. Given a superficial reading of the text, there is really no reason for them to do otherwise. To arrive at the conclusion that the latecomers were Gentiles, one would have to know something about the theological and political crises confronting the early church as it expanded its mission throughout the Roman Empire. However, once we are forced—by additional data—to identify ourselves with the latecomers, the story takes on a completely different cast. Instead of feeling irritated and confused by an apparent miscarriage of justice, we are likely to feel a profound sense of gratitude for ever having been called to work in the vineyard in the first place! This change of "location" in the story results in a radical change in meaning, raising a host of new questions about the meaning of justice and mercy.

Similarly, the parable of the tax-collector (or "publican") and the Pharisee (Luke 18:9-14) provides another striking example of what happens when, *as a result of new information,* we find ourselves "somewhere else" in the story. This story, as told by Jesus, clearly condemns the self-righteous Pharisee—a man we instantly dislike, in spite of the fact that the good works he recounts (fasting twice a week and giving tithes of everything he purchased) show that he was willing to do far more than the Law actually required of him. (The Law required only one fast a year, and normally much of what he would purchase would have been tithed already by the producer.)

Christians who (thanks to Paul) commonly refer to themselves "sinners" almost always tend to identify themselves with the repentant tax-collector, who also labels himself a "sinner." Yet this rather facile identification generally overlooks the fact that the Jewish tax-collector of first-century Palestine was, by almost any definition, a "crook." The taxes he collected were levied by a hated colonial power, so that in carrying out his job, he was seen by loyal Jews to be a "quisling" or collaborator with the enemy. In most cases tax-collectors took advantage of their authority, systematically extorting more from helpless Jewish peasants than was their due. So despised were tax-collectors that they were barred from holding communal office or from giving testimony in court; and even the rabbis considered it ethical to cheat them! Like the harlot with whom he was continually lumped by the Gospel writers, the tax-collector was a person whose integrity was "for sale."

The Gospel accounts assume all this. Their original audiences would have understood immediately why the tax-collector was distraught, just as they would have been profoundly shocked to hear that Jesus included a member of this profession among his chosen disciples. The twentieth-century reader is dependent on the efforts of Bible scholars who make this information available in Bible dictionaries, commentaries, and other reference works.[2] Once we are in possession of this information, the tax-collector's cry, "God, be merciful to me a sinner!" takes on added force. This man really was a "miserable sinner," a person who deliberately chose to live outside of Israel's covenantal relationship with God. The community's requirements for a return to a regularized relationship were harsh and probably impossible to fulfill: The offending party was to locate every person he had cheated for the purpose of repaying the amount extorted plus an extra fifth!

The tendency of sincere, "God-fearing" Christians to identify themselves with the "sinner" of this parable is, quite simply, wrong. With the exception of the converted criminal (including the white-collar variety) most church members and Bible students—while they may not be as generous with their worldly goods—are much closer in spirit and circumstance to the Pharisee, who is being more than faithful to the terms of the covenant as he understands them. The plight of most of us law-abiding "sinners" may be grave, but it is not particularly analogous to that of the tax-collector and, if we are honest, we will admit to being glad that this is the case!

Again, we are faced with a situation where a change of

"place" in the story radically alters our understanding of it and forces us to deal with a different set of questions. The justification in this parable of a man of such questionable morals—in contrast to the faithful Pharisee—requires that all honest people of faith take a second look at their own stance toward law-breakers. Are "sinners" such as those described by Luke to be equated with "sinners" as Paul uses this term? Is this parable telling us that a sacrificial life-style (such as that of the Pharisee) does not really matter after all? Or, if we are not to be grateful that *we* are not law-breakers, then for what should we be grateful? Ironically, the parable of the tax-collector and the Pharisee, which most Christians find comforting and attractive, should actually be understood as confronting. And conversely, the parable of the laborers in the vineyard, which many people find so annoying, is better understood as a word of radical hope to those who feel most annoyed! In each case, exegetical study changes our understanding not only of what the passage may have meant to the original audience but also of what it may mean for us today—and more often than not the impact of this change of perspective is jarring. Suddenly scripture is saying something new and surprising to us. Can we hear what is being said and act on it?

To What End Do We Study?

Few of us can afford the luxury of study for its own sake; we study to achieve some practical goal. The justification for a careful exegesis of the biblical text is the faith community's need to *locate itself accurately* in the story. We need to hear what the text as "Word of God" is saying to *us*. In theory, the church has always maintained that the study of scripture is an essential component of discipleship. In practice, its efforts to support the serious study of the Bible have generally been faltering.

Every Christian realizes that he or she is supposed to know something about the Bible, that somehow scripture is meant to be both formative and normative for a Christian life-style; yet access to the Word of God remains blocked for many people. The truly remarkable thing is that the *desire* to study scripture persists in the face of so many repeated failures and frustrations! Out of a sense of obedience and love the church continues to struggle to find new ways to make scripture accessible, for the conviction remains that (somehow, somewhere) there is a Word from God for us *now* and that it can and should make a difference in the way we lead our lives.

The question that confronts us all as members of the body of Christ is not, Will the study of scripture show us *how* to change our lives? nor is it even, Will the study of scripture make us *want* to change our lives? The situation we face is more desperate than this, the question more haunting. What we need to know is *whether the study of scripture itself actually will change our lives:* Does the power to convert, to change, to transform wasted lives reside in what the church calls the Word of God, and can that power be appropriated through a sustained and disciplined encounter with the biblical texts?

We have all had the experience of opening the Bible at random, searching in vain for something inspiring. We have also had the experience of having a passage from scripture speak immediately and powerfully to a situation we were facing, whether in a comforting or confronting way. At such times we are indeed convinced that scripture is the Word of God, and we wonder why it doesn't always seem to be so. Unfortunately, there is no sure-fire formula for guaranteeing that every time we open the Bible we will experience instant succor or feel convicted of our sins; conversion and change are ultimately the work of the Holy Spirit. Nevertheless, we can learn a little more about the conditions under which this type of direct and compelling encounter is likely to take place.

The Conversion of the Exegete: Becoming Like Children

To begin with, I would suggest that our prayers for guidance and inspiration should also, in some sense, be petitions for conversion, for the grace to change. Exegesis is a powerful tool in the hand of its practitioner, and the blessings it brings are not always unmixed. Inherent in all its possibilities are pitfalls of which the church must always be aware. The change we seek as a result of our study is not the kind of change that will allow us to objectify or manipulate God's word and distance ourselves from it. The change we seek is a more total

involvement in God's word—a change that may be characterized as a return to the eager and innocent stance a child
assumes in relation to a well-loved story. This is not to say that
we should suspend our critical faculties or abandon our efforts
to recover more information about the historical circumstances that gave rise to the text. Responsible exegesis always
provides a reliable point of entry into the biblical material; but
exegesis *in itself* does not release the power of the Word so that
it may become active in our lives. What does? I believe that the
stance of the child toward the story provides us with an
important clue, and this stance is characterized by at least two
things: anticipation and identification.

a. *Anticipation and Change:* Consider what happens when
children read or listen to a story: They sit in rapt attention,
blocking out everything else around them. The child seated
before a good storyteller experiences a strong, almost exultant
sense of anticipation. She expects something wonderful to
happen *to her* and prepares herself accordingly. In fact
something actually will happen to her (and perhaps change the
way in which she sees the world) because of the manner in
which she participates in that story's special reality. The
retelling of the same story over and over again is generally no
obstacle to the child's enjoyment of it, for the child's
imagination feeds on these retellings, just as her body grows as
a result of a sound diet.

In much the same way, and while still a very young nation,
Israel told and retold important stories—not simply because
they were interesting in themselves (which they were) but
because the expectation was there that in the retelling there
was also a "reliving" and that the saving power of which the
story spoke could be experienced again in a present situation
of need. Israel recognized that without a gracious Word from
God "now" no real change or conversion was possible.

But what do we as adults anticipate as we prepare ourselves
to read a familiar text or listen to the Sunday lections? When
the minister announces that the text for the sermon will be the
parable of the good Samaritan are we excited at the prospect?
Aren't we more likely to say to ourselves, "I *know* that
story—what can possibly be said now that hasn't already been
said countless times before?" The point, of course, of good

biblical preaching is to allow us to hear the text as though for the first time, just as the point of retelling stories to children (who seem actually to relish the repetition) is to enable them to experience something that is pleasurable and instructive at increasingly deeper levels of comprehension. The difference is that the expectant attitude of the child puts both child and storyteller at an advantage. By contrast, the preacher working with familiar Bible passages and passive adults is at a distinct disadvantage!

b. *Identification and Change:* All children know that the stories they hear and read are really *about them,* and that, of course, is what makes children's books so wonderful and powerful. Each child listening to a story quickly identifies him or herself with the hero or heroine; any details not supplied by the author are promptly supplied by the listener, who, if asked, will tell you precisely what the princess was wearing or describe the wicked witch in terms that resemble the crabby old lady who lives down the block.

A similar but more conscious kind of identification occurs whenever the Passover liturgy is performed in Jewish households. For countless generations Jews have been exhorted to remember the Exodus event as something *they themselves* experienced: "Not only our ancestors alone did the Holy One redeem but *us* as well, along with them, as it is written: 'And he freed *us* from Egypt . . .'"[3] Through this deliberate identification the modern Jew continues to participate in the Exodus event and thus re-appropriates it for the present generation. Implicit in the affirmation that God frees *us* from Egypt is the belief that what God did for our ancestors, he can do for us today!

What happens in the celebration of the Passover should not be construed as an attempt to magically repeat history. Instead, it should be understood as a recognition that, *under certain circumstances,* people of faith can overcome the barrier of the centuries and invoke the same power that first parted the waters of the sea as a means of deliverance. Under *which* circumstances?

This invocation is legitimate and effective when the one remembering the saving event is experiencing what one Bible scholar refers to as the same "quality of time,"[4] i.e., when the one remembering has made an *accurate identification* in relation to the biblical material, recognizing that in some way the human dilemma and divine response described in scripture are analogous to what he or she is experiencing. (The experience of the black church in their use of Exodus imagery during the Civil Rights Movement provides us with a classic example of how this kind of legitimate identification and re-appropriation takes place.)

Unfortunately, most adults have difficulty in understanding that the Bible is also a book about *them*. Part of this difficulty is due to the generally impoverished state of the average adult's imagination. We are not so adept at supplying the details! Equally, if not more problematic is our awareness of the immense distance that separates the world we inhabit from that of Jeremiah or Jesus. We know just enough to realize that these worlds *are* vastly different from one another, and so we hesitate (quite rightly) to supply details that might be not only inadequate but utterly incorrect!

Fortunately, exegetical study provides an effective corrective for this type of problem. For example, one of the first things a new exegete learns is that what is familiar is not necessarily known nor understood. The riches to be mined in even a single verse of scripture are a matter of much astonishment: a little additional reading about one key word can yield a host of new insights or suggest many other questions to pursue.

The practiced exegete has learned that an essential part of the discipline of study is recognizing and avoiding the trap of overconfidence when dealing with especially familiar material. The study of Scripture must be undertaken with the understanding that there will always be more to learn about the passage in question; to assume that we already "know" what it says or means is to risk assuming that God has nothing new to say to us now. The effort expended in study will almost certainly produce a change in our understanding of a passage—that we can expect. What is more important, a change of understanding presents us with new possibilities for personal and corporate change. That we *must* expect.

The wealth of new detail we uncover through exegesis provides a powerful stimulus to our imaginations, making it possible for us to participate in what we read at deeper emotional levels; but the special strength of exegesis is that while it nurtures the imagination, it also *disciplines* it by establishing basic parameters beyond which the stimulated imagination may not go. Through practice we become increasingly sensitive to the problems encountered—and to the kind of serious damage that can be done—when, without respect for these limits, one hastily and carelessly interprets biblical material. At the very least, we learn to distinguish between the informed guess and pure speculation!

c. *The Requirements of Change:* It is a relatively easy thing to talk about practices and attitudes that facilitate change, particularly when we are thinking in very positive terms about "change," i.e., about renewal, rebirth, growth, or development. After all, isn't this what "conversion" means?

Our English word "convert" is taken from the Latin *convertere,* which means to turn, turn about, or transform. (In the Bible the Hebrew *shub* and Greek *strepho* are both translated "turn," "return," or "convert.") The notion of change as progress or growth does not really express the radical reorientation implied by the word "conversion." The kind of turning implied by conversion is a dramatic change of heart, mind, and life. It is just as often a turning *back* to someone or thing as it is a pushing off into new directions.

The decision to initiate a sustained dialogue with scripture marks a *re*turning to ancient sources of meaning and identity. The dynamics of this encounter, however, are not always pleasant or affirming. The community that converts to active dialogue with scripture will find itself up against assertions and faith claims that may first of all make them feel uncomfortable and second provoke feelings of inadequacy, amazement, or even anger. Why? Because, in exegesis, scripture's "first word" has a power and a primacy that it does not normally have in more casual encounters. Claim what they may, most churches, including the most conservative, are accustomed to *using* scripture as a tool or resource; exegesis requires that we (at least initially) *submit* ourselves to the biblical agenda and adjust our own agendas accordingly. Accustomed as we are to making claims for the Bible, it is always jolting to experience and respond to the strong claims the Bible makes on us!

The careful and objective study of texts that is required if we are to locate ourselves accurately in the story often has surprising, quite unintended consequences. What happens, for instance, when the "place" in which we find ourselves turns out to be an untenable or indefensible position? What happens when the change required of us turns out to be painful, humiliating, or sacrificial? *Can* we change under those circumstances? *Must* we change?

The answer to the first question—Can we change?—is almost certainly yes. God does not require of us tasks that are impossible to fulfill, though the effort may involve risk and therefore require great courage. Scripture witnesses to God's faithfulness in fully equipping those who are called to transform themselves and their communities. Indeed, the desire to be *faithful above all else* assumes a readiness to continually change or be changed in painful as well as glorious ways.

The second question—Must we change?—is far harder to answer, for it hinges on yet another question, that of the *authority* of scripture. Created in freedom, we have been given the option to say no to the invitation to change. Ultimately, our response to this invitation will depend on how much weight the Word of God is seen to carry in our individual and corporate lives. Each time we hear a word of either hope or judgment from scripture we are faced with the toughest questions of all: Do you believe it? or, Can you accept in faith what you cannot freely believe?

CHAPTER NINE

First and Last Words:

Dealing with Different Perspectives on Biblical Authority

So shall my word be that goes forth
    from my mouth;
  it shall not return to me empty,
but it shall accomplish that which I
    purpose,
  and prosper in the thing for which
    I sent it.

Isaiah 55:11

The Unpleasant Reality

Among Christians of every description the Bible is considered in *some* way authoritative. It is the repository of the faith, the treasury of tradition, the ultimate guide to the good life. Yet this universally high regard for scripture is reflected in a bewildering diversity of opinion as to precisely *what* faith, *what* traditions, and *what* rules are proclaimed in its pages. Further, there is no consensus on the problem of what difference all this should make in the life of the individual believer or the church. Alternately adored and ignored, the Bible remains a source of conflict and confusion among Christians, a stumbling block of immense proportions.

1. *The Substitution of Claims for Content:* Granting pride of place to the Bible has not contributed substantially to Christian unity on the subject of scripture. In fact, the more people talk *about* the Bible, the more likely they are to disagree, for talking

about the Bible usually involves making claims either for or against it. Ask a group of people to fill in the blank for the following sentence: "The Bible is _____." Invariably, every response will contain a value judgment, for the Bible is not something about which we can remain neutral. The most popular response is "God's Word." Other favorites include "inerrant," "infallible," "inspired," "important," "irrelevant," or "mostly myth." By and large, it is the nature of the claims we make for scripture rather than scripture itself that causes the conflict. Unfortunately, the majority of people who make strong claims either for or against the Bible know relatively little about its actual contents, for its is much easier to claim that the Bible is inerrant or irrelevant than it is to spend time comparing and contrasting parallel accounts of the same event in Matthew, Mark, and Luke. What happens, of course, when we actually *study* the Bible with some regularity and rigor is that our claims for it—no matter what they may be—are first tested and then modified. Therefore the prospect of a sustained dialogue with scripture presents us with some serious problems, aside from the purely logistical ones: *Nobody* relishes the experience of being challenged to the point of having to change one's premises, prejudices, or behavior.

Roman Catholics are to be credited with having understood all along the explosive power of the scriptures. In an excess of caution the church kept the Bible "under wraps" for centuries, maintaining (first) that scripture was the work of the church and (second) that *only* the church, i.e., the clergy, was competent to interpret scripture. Since Vatican II, Catholicism has intentionally sought to "unwrap" the scriptures and, ironically, recent Roman Catholic biblical scholarship has been one of the most effective and empowering developments in the continuing search for Christian unity. In the world of scholarly research, Roman Catholic and Protestant authorities have collaborated to produce valuable studies on biblical topics related to areas of doctrinal controversies. The results of these joint efforts are impressive in their own right, but perhaps their real significance lies in their demonstration that Christians from different denominational backgrounds, heirs of traditions that make strikingly different claims about scripture, can find much to agree on when the biblical witness is allowed to speak for itself.[1]

The Protestant Reformation tore open the wrappings, severing the clergy's tight hold on access to scripture and matters of biblical interpretation. Instead of remaining a resource reserved for the more or less exclusive use of the clergy, the Bible became the "church's book" in a far fuller sense. The Reformers believed that the Bible was *the* standard against which all change in the church should be measured. Their goal was to get the vernacular Bible into the hands of every lay man and woman with the assumption, quite naturally, that once possessed, the Bible would be *read*. Unfortunately, the liberation of scripture (in this partial sense) has resulted in an indefensible fragmentation of the church and its faith—a fragmentation that is largely the result of conflicting *claims* about the appropriate role of scripture in the life of the church.

Most ironically, there is today relatively little (if any) discernible difference between the biblical expertise of the average mainstream Protestant and Roman Catholic layperson. Both are more or less innocent of knowledge of the Bible's actual content. The substitution of claims about the Bible for a knowledge of biblical content is only one consequence of this general neglect; another is the near universal resort to convenient categories or labels that are mostly used to discredit Christians whose claims for scripture conflict with our own.

2. *Libelous Labels:* The problem of biblical interpretation and authority might be less troublesome if we, as adults, *did* come "naked" and innocent to biblical texts, ready to hear the word as if for the first time. Instead, we come "clothed" with layers of previous experiences, jaundiced with memories of bad sermons and boring Sunday school classes. We carry as baggage histories of previous (usually mediated) involvement with scripture which prejudice our reaction to the passage under consideration. Thus equipped, we are ready at a moment's notice to offer an interpretation that mirrors our biases. Few of us are aware, however, to what extent our responses to scripture are conditioned by a previously chosen orientation toward the church in general and toward scripture in particular. These orientations are conveniently and

simplistically labeled for purposes of instant recognition. The broadest and most easily abused labels are "conservative" and "liberal."

Incredibly handy, these labels are nonetheless pernicious in their impact, since they are so often used to discredit someone else's point of view. For example, when a self-designated liberal refers to a person as "conservative" what she most often means is that this person can be expected to claim that scripture is inerrant (at least in matters of faith). The stereotypical conservative also stands accused by the liberal of first *spiritualizing* the biblical message (i.e., severing its message from its human or historical context) and then *personalizing* it by applying it strictly to the individual Christian when in fact the Bible is a document addressed to faith communities. On the other hand, ask a self-designated conservative to describe a "liberal," and you will likely hear charges that liberals neither know nor believe in the Bible, that they make use of it in a highly selective and cynical way, i.e., when it can be made to serve their *political* interests, and that they willfully ignore the New Testament emphasis on individual salvation. "Vague," "wishy-washy," and "secular-humanist" are the standard adjectives used to describe the liberal stance. (Persons who use labels in this pejorative sense will often resent the use of anything other than denominational labels for him or herself: "*I* am a Presbyterian, Methodist, Catholic . . .") An additional and particularly destructive use of labels is the recent reservation of the word "Christian" by and for persons who claim to have been "born again." This specialized use (or abuse) of the term tends to be coupled with a strictly literalistic view of scripture so that one frequently hears the charge that persons who do not accept a creationist theory of the origins of the universe are not "Christian." When used in this way labels set up a series of expectations not only about an individual, a congregation, or a denomination, but also about ways of reading, studying, and interpreting scripture—expectations that make mutual dialogue or shared study between "liberals" and "conservatives" almost impossible.

Now the positions mentioned above are certainly caricatures. No self-respecting conservative or liberal would accept these characterizations as fair or accurate. But it is also a fact that persons who use the "conservative" label to describe themselves in a *positive* way do tend to use personal or individualistic categories in interpreting scripture, just as self-designated "liberals" prefer collective categories because of a predetermined position that the political and social implications of scripture are *at least* as important as the issue of individual salvation, if not more so. Predictably, both liberals and conservatives invariably seek out persons of similar persuasions for purposes of group study and reflection, so that Bible study groups and classes frequently bear the stamp of one orientation toward critical method or the other and are merely self-ratifying in their impact. This form of ideological exclusivity which insists on seeing the other point of view as *competing instead of complementary* victimizes the church and its scriptures. This is the unpleasant reality in which we find ourselves.

In Dialogue with Our Faith Traditions

Locked into unsatisfactory positions by confining labels, we tend to see ourselves as trapped in a peculiarly modern predicament. In earlier, "simpler," and less secular times there was, we assume, a consensus that accepted a straightforward literal interpretation of scripture. Untroubled by scientific world view and high technology, the church was spared elaborate intellectual attempts to demythologize the Bible. Nothing could be further from the truth.

In fact the lines for today's "Battle for the Bible" were drawn as early as the second century A.D. Christian exegetes who were influenced primarily by *Jewish* biblical scholarship generally espoused a literal reading of scripture which assumed its historical accuracy and included a healthy respect for questions of context. At the same time these interpreters (referred to by historians as the School of Antioch) were not exclusively concerned with the Bible's literal sense: they were equally concerned to interpret scripture at a level that transcended its historical-literal dimension. Furthermore, they did not hesitate to appeal to extra-biblical traditions of apostolic teaching for help in clarifying ambiguous or difficult biblical material. This school of thought judged scripture to be reliable and true on the basis of its conformity to orthodox

Christian doctrine or the "rule of faith." Scripture judged the church, but it was the church who decided what was scriptural; and at this point the church was still involved in the process of assessing the value and authority of *many* Christian documents, only some of which finally became scriptural. Although modified in many respects, the historical-literal approach to biblical exegesis has remained the central exegetical tradition of orthodox Christianity.

Elsewhere, a school of equally learned biblical scholars were rejecting as *non*historical large portions of scripture while simultaneously conferring total authority and reliability on *all* of scripture. Trained as philosophers and rhetoricians, these scholars were the products of *Greek* modes of higher education, and their intellectual backgrounds made it impossible for them to accept of all of scripture as literally true or factually accurate. Surprisingly, lack of historical reliability was seen as no obstacle to a very exalted view of biblical authority. Factual or not, scripture was completely reliable and "true." Then what, one may ask, was their standard of "truth"? Obviously, it was not a matter of what could be scientifically documented. The truth of scripture, according to this school of thought, rested in its profound spiritual or symbolic significance. Virtually every passage—no matter how mundane or problematic, contained a hidden message for the Christian. This allegorical method of exegesis (from the Greek *allegoria,* meaning "speaking otherwise") is associated in particular with Christian scholars from Alexandria, Egypt, an early center not only of Greek erudition but of Christian culture as well.

The most famous of the allegorical expositors was the Alexandrian Origen (A.D. 185–254). A man of exceptional intellectual powers, Origen's interest in the Bible became evident at a very early age. The church historian Eusebius tells the following story:

> In addition to putting him through the usual educational curriculum his father was very anxious that [Origen] should learn about the Bible. . . . Every day he would set him to learn passages by heart and then give an account of what he had learned. The child complied without the slightest reluctance; in fact he went about it too enthusiastically; he was not content with the straightforward,

obvious meaning of the scriptures; he wanted something more, and even at that time would go in pursuit of the underlying sense.[2]

Practically speaking, Origen devoted his entire life to the Bible, developing a method of text criticism, writing commentaries and delivering homilies on scripture, and producing reams of notes on difficult passages. Legendary for his teaching skills, Origen had pupils flock to him; wherever he went, centers of Christian learning developed. Significantly, the foundation of this enormous intellectual and emotional investment in scripture was a passionate regard for the Bible's ultimate *authority*.

The modern mind finds Origen's problems with a more literal interpretation of scripture quite baffling and even unnecessary. Origen seems not to have been bothered by accounts of miraculous events in which the laws of nature are suspended; rather, the subtler (and more mundane) discrepancies in such things as parallel passages in the Gospels worried him. For example, very slight variations in wording in parallel passages were known to drive him to distraction! Origen is not bothered, for example, by Jesus' extraordinary claims to divinity in the Gospel of John. Instead, he is troubled by the fact that John's Gospel places the story of the cleansing of the temple at the *beginning* of Jesus' ministry instead of at the end as the Synoptic Gospels do. Even the story itself—an account most moderns take delight in because of its very human and political dimensions—Origen finds quite *un*believable. The radical nature of Jesus' violent response to commercial trafficking in the temple is entirely unaccountable! How could the son of a lowly carpenter, Origen asks, "venture upon such an act as to drive out a crowd of merchants from the temple?" The act described is, on the face of it, a gesture of incredible arrogance: "And did not Jesus do an unwarrantable thing when he poured out the money of the moneychangers . . . ?" Surely if anyone actually had been beaten by Jesus he would certainly have fought back! "Does it not bespeak audacity and temerity and even some measure of lawlessness?" For Origen, this story is "true" because its meaning lies *elsewhere* than in the surface sense of the passage. Jesus' purging of the temple is actually a continual purging of his church in which corrupt elements are always to be found. At another level, this account reveals that the time of animal sacrifices and the observance of Mosaic law had come to an end; in fact, the "coins" of the moneychangers are not really coins at all but the Law "which appears so venerable." Finally, at an even deeper level, Origen could claim that the temple is really the "soul," which Jesus disciplines with the "whip" of his Word.[5]

Origen was always controversial, and eventually his extreme method of allegorical exegesis was discredited by the church. More recently, his contribution to biblical scholarship has been undergoing reassessment, for it is clear that he influenced countless other biblical expositors. Meanwhile, the search for "deeper" meanings in scripture, though it now takes different forms, continues. (In fact, all those who seek an *a*historical, "spiritual" meaning in scripture are the heirs of Origen's legacy.) The "correctness" or lack thereof of Origen's exegetical method is really of secondary interest, however. In the context of his times, Origen is to be credited with having opened the door of the church to other intellectuals like himself, among them no less a luminary than Saint Augustine, Bishop of Hippo.

Aurelius Augustinus (A.D. 354–430), originally a convert of a heretical (and extremely literalistic) Christian sect, was attracted to orthodox Christianity while still a relatively young man. Unfortunately, it was a matter of *years* before Augustine was able to embrace the faith fully and be baptized. A significant obstacle for Augustine was the Old Testament, which he had been taught to understand with a rigid literalism. As a brilliant young scholar, Augustine felt forced to reject the Old Testament as nothing but a collection of crude myths and morally objectionable material. If becoming a Christian meant having to believe *that* was God's Word, then—no matter how much he might wish it—such a thing was never meant to be! For Augustine, the door of the church seemed slammed shut. Providentially, Augustine was given the opportunity to hear Ambrose, the Bishop of Milan, preach. Ambrose was eloquent, and, like Origen, Ambrose interpreted scripture *allegorically*.

In his autobiography Augustine explains that he listened to Ambrose explain, one after another, the "hard places of the Old Testament—passages that "had been death to me when I took them literally, but once I had heard them explained in their spiritual meaning I began to blame myself for my despair."[4] This experience marked a significant turning point in Augustine's journey toward conversion. The door that had been shut now began to swing open.

The kind of spiritualizing interpretation of scripture practiced by Origen and Ambrose is rejected by today's biblical theologians whose concern is with the literal sense (if not the historical accuracy) of biblical texts. Yet we need to recognize that, in its day, allegorical interpretation proved an effective way of reaching people whose educational backgrounds required a different sort of introduction to the Bible. Like many other highly educated converts, Augustine was to find that the issue of literalism faded in importance as he dealt with scripture as a resource for preaching and teaching in a pastoral context. Augustine implicitly accepted the authority of scripture: he came to *believe* it to be "true" in every sense of the word—and he *believed* this—as he said—in order that he might someday *understand*. Like those biblical scholars who preceded and followed him, Augustine made full use of all the scholarly assistance available at the time and scorned those who felt they could interpret scripture in a purely personal way without the assistance of any human aid.

Centuries later the church was forced to focus its attention on scripture in a dramatic way as the Reformers sought to alter its relationship to the church. Placing the church completely "under" the judgment of scripture, they nevertheless developed their own systems for evaluating the authority of scripture in general and scriptures in particular. For Martin Luther (1483–1546), those portions of scripture which "preached Christ" had primacy over those which did not. In practice, this meant, for example, that Paul's words carried more weight than James'. Luther granted that it was desirable to have an appreciation of the historical situation of the biblical author, but at the same time he claimed that the Bible was not a difficult book to understand since its meaning was self-evident. In theory, every literate person, peasant or prince, should be able to read and interpret scripture. In practice, Luther devoted considerable time to the writing of biblical commentary!

John Calvin (1509–1564) postulated a much more objective

authority for scripture than did Luther. He assumed that if the Bible is "divine," then its words must be construed as carrying the same weight of authority as if they were pronounced by God himself. Yet no one could prove this authority by rational argument; only a prior faith or the inward testimony of the Spirit could make possible such a radical view of biblical authority. And although Calvin believed faith was essential to a proper understanding of scripture, he never asserted that faith relieves us of the responsibility of using scholarly tools as an aid to accurate exegesis. Trained rigorously in classics and the law, Calvin studied biblical texts with scrupulous objectivity and with a strong concern for identifying the author's intention as well as contextual issues.

Taking the Long View

No cursory treatment such as this can do real justice to the long, complex, and fascinating story of the church's involvement with scripture; yet even a *little* exposure to that history gives us reason to pause and reevaluate our too simple and long-cherished assumptions about the *nature* of that relationship. The average layperson is blissfully unaware of the extent to which disagreements about the nature of biblical authority have permeated the church's history—so much so that it would appear that this is truly a *human* problem and not merely a historical one. (Is it possible that there *never was* a time when it was "easier" to believe the witness of scripture than it is now?) The discovery that "our" problems are not unique and that some of the greatest leaders the church has ever known had similar problems to deal with is, at the very least, humbling. Some would say it is heartening—heartening because taking a long view of the problem inevitably alters our perspective and offers us the chance to profit from the lessons of history.

1. *How History Helps:* The simplest and most obvious lesson we learn from history is that the debate over the issue of biblical literalism is as old as the church itself and that it surfaced as soon as the Bible became an authoritative document for people other than the Jews (this is not to mention divisions among learned rabbis). The chances are good, therefore, that if the problem has been with us this long, it's likely to *remain* with us. Those of us

who believe that people can be made to change from one position to another through force of rational argument, or even as a result of a conversion experience, are at best naïve.

To begin with, we know that there are many people today—especially young people—who react to scripture in precisely the same way as Augustine: they find its unscientific world view crude and repugnant. To say to such people, "If you don't believe that the world was created in six twenty-four hour periods, you cannot be a real Christian," is to make the Bible a stumbling block on the road to faith instead of a lamp casting light on the truth-seeker's path.

On the other hand, many other people have precisely the opposite problem. If what we call "God's Word" cannot be considered at least potentially scientifically verifiable, then it cannot also be "true." If it is not "true" in this sense, it may not be true in other respects either, so that the entire witness of scripture, including its theological positions, is called into question. A historical-critical stance, which stresses the time and culture-conditioned qualities of the Bible, threatens to erode the authority of scripture whenever people feel compelled to apply the same rational-critical standards to scripture that they would to modern scientific and historical documents to determine "reliability." An attitude that refuses to take this problem for faith seriously is equally "closed" and divisive.

In the second place, history tells us that the church has been "fed" and nourished by leaders who sat on both sides of the fence. Furthermore, the views of these great theologians about the *historical* reliability of scripture did not appear to be the determining factor in inspiring either their respect for the Bible's authority or their devotion to it in terms of the commitment of time and energy. Factual or not, scripture was understood to be inspired, reliable, and "true"—at least at one or more symbolical levels. The contemporary habit of relying on historical accuracy as the *chief* indicator of reliability and worth evidences a lack of confidence in the inspiration of scripture and a lack of respect for the freedom of the God who speaks through scripture. And this is just as true for persons who *reject* the Bible on this basis as for those who accept it.

Third, history tells us that the church's great thinkers were all thoroughly acquainted with the contents of scripture. Their view of the appropriate role of scripture necessitated a substantial investment of time to the effort of study. In short, they knew their Bible well! At the same time, it is obvious that all of them were products of particular—and therefore *limiting*—social, educational, and religious milieus. Their exegetical practices reflect the academic standards and methodologies of *their* day—and not ours. But by skillfully applying these methodologies, theologians were able to deal creatively and forcefully with biblical texts in ways that spoke directly to the deep human and spiritual needs of their audiences.

Finally, history tells us that whether the Bible was seen primarily as the source of the church or its product, its formal (and actual) authority always demonstrated a vital, intense, and ongoing relationship with the church. In either sense, the Bible has remained the "church's book," for (historically speaking) the church has been the context for Bible study, the focus of Bible study, and the justification for Bible study. The Bible's major interpreters have always combined their study with activity that ultimately clarified, renewed, reformed, or otherwise challenged the direction in which the People of God were moving.

2. *How Theology Helps: Asking the Questions That Count:* Those expositors of scripture whose work lives on beyond them to actually change minds and hearts dealt with scripture at a level that cannot be accurately labeled either "historical" or "spiritual" but (for lack of a better word) must be termed "theological."

The word "theology" is derived from the Greek *theologos* (theos = God; logos = word or discourse). In a formal or technical sense, the word refers to the academic study of a system of religious beliefs about God, creation, sin, salvation, and so forth. Broadly speaking, theological questions are questions of *meaning* and *relationship* dealt with in the context of a set of religious beliefs. (See also chapter 7, pp. 143-45.) In the context of biblical study, theological questions force us to deal directly wih questions about the nature of God, God's relationship to the created order, our relationships to one another, and the nature and work of Jesus Christ. All biblical material relates to questions such as these *at least indirectly,* and this is the case no matter how questionable the material may be historically. To illustrate this, let us look at one of the most powerful and problematic stories in the Bible—the story of Jonah.

The book of Jonah is often used as one of those acid tests which separates "believers" from "nonbelievers." What happens when the issue for discussion is, Was Jonah really swallowed by a whale?—or "great fish" as the text has it. Or, Could a human being really survive for three days and nights under those conditions? Or, Can God do *anything*? In the first place, only the last question can rightly be called a "theological" question; the first two questions are better described as historical (Did it actually occur?) and scientific (Could it actually occur?). The question, Can God do anything? may be legitimately asked in relation to the story of Jonah, but in theological (or *relational*) terms it is best directed to the repentance of the Ninevites or Jonah's success as a preacher (i.e., how miraculous were *these* events? What do they tell us about the nature of God?) Do we then dismiss the whale altogether? Certainly not. We cannot understand the story fully without asking what *function* the whale plays in relation to God's purposes and in relation to Jonah and his response to God. Is the whale a form of punishment or deliverance? What interests the storyteller about the whale—its size or its instrumentality? What does Jonah *do* during those three dark days and nights? Does this action give us a clue to how the writer views the function of the great fish? What is the *primary* focus of the writer's attention: Jonah's miraculous delivery or Jonah's struggle with God? What is the book of Jonah *really about*?

Questions about relationship and meaning in the biblical texts can—and in most instances should—be dealt with without reference to their possible facticity, for in the last analysis, these are the questions that count. People who wish—or need—to believe that the story is factual will *not* be convinced by the arguments of nonbelievers and vice versa. People's need to believe or disbelieve is rooted in something too deep for mere logic, and even if this were not the case, there will never be sufficient data either to prove or disprove the historical nature of the biblical narratives to anyone's satisfaction.

Therefore, *it is fruitless and destructive to focus attention and discussion around purely historical or scientific issues in the context of congregational Bible study.* History or legend, the story of Jonah is perversely accurate in its portrayal of a God who, sooner or later, requires us to minister to those whom we hate—or a God who insists on showing mercy when what *we* are calling for is vengeance.

3. *Does History Help with Theology?* To say that biblical texts should be dealt with at a *theological* level is not the same thing as saying that they should be "spiritualized" or cut loose from their historical moorings. With the exception of the wisdom literature (which is itself a product of peculiar historical and cultural developments), the Bible is self-consciously "historical" in the presentation of its message. By this I mean that biblical narratives are set in identifiable historical situations: the Abraham stories contain details which reflect the patriarchal period, just as the Gospels recount stories about Jesus and his disciples in relation to a people who were suffering under colonial overrule.

It is important to remember, however, that the historical setting of a narrative does not necessarily correspond to the historical circumstances of the biblical writer. For example, Genesis was written long after the events it describes; and we can be quite sure that much later *events would have had some impact on the choice of material included and the kinds of theological questions raised.* As we have indicated before, examination of these factors is a standard part of exegetical study. It is also necessary to be clear that in acknowledging the importance of historical settings and circumstances *we are not at the same time insisting that the Bible provide us with an objective account of actual historical events;* that is another issue altogether. Rather, the exegete is interested in the "historical" setting of the biblical narrative and the myriad of little details that create this setting for the simple reason that this information helps sharpen and clarify what is at stake *theologically.*

What the Bible witnesses to is a God who chose to relate himself to a very particular (and motley!) group of slaves and nomads who lived long ago in ways we would find incredibly primitive and with rules we would find unbearably stifling and rigid. The Bible does not often speak of grace and deliverance or election in general but mostly of *particular* grace (the ram caught in the thicket), *particular* deliverance (a path through the Red Sea), and *particular* election (the unlikely choice of the rogue Jacob and his descendants as "Israel"). Theologizing that flows from biblical material—and ultimately all theological discourse is somehow rooted in scripture—cannot be cut loose from the *specifics* of sin and grace, of deliverance and destruction. We cannot speak of a Christ apart from the first-century Nazarene; we cannot speak of callings without reference to the called, to Moses, Jeremiah, and Mary. In short, we cannot ignore the historical terms *that the text takes as a given* and then proceed to interpret the text without reference to them.

Take Jonah—again. Jonah is not *any* man; he is an Israelite. And he is not called to preach repentance to *any* nation; he is called to preach to the inhabitants of Ninevah, the capital of the Assyrian empire. How important are these specifics to understanding what is at stake theologically? They are vitally important.

For over one hundred fifty years Assyria menaced both the northern kingdom of Israel and the southern kingdom of Judah. Eventually Assyrian troups demolished the northern kingdom, leading away captive many of the inhabitants who were never again to return. Assyrian warriors, perhaps the most vicious the ancient Near East was ever to produce, were feared and despised by Israel. A call from God to "preach repentance" to such as these could hardly be met with enthusiasm! To Jonah it must have seemed not only inscrutable but insane. God's willingness to show mercy to the Ninevites is, under these circumstances, baffling and infuriating.

The circumstances, the details *do* matter. They show us just how high the stakes really were for Jonah. They help us understand why he was so determined to run away from this call and why he bitterly resented his own success as a preacher of repentance. The choice of Israel's most hated foe as the object of God's special mercy is what makes this story "true" in the deepest sense of the word and therefore theologically significant. A fruitful study of the book of Jonah will therefore be based on two things—things on which both liberals and conservatives ought to be able to agree:

1) A thorough knowledge of the *contents* of the book (based on an exegetical examination of the text using standard reference tools); and
2) A focus on the *theological* issues addressed in the text rather than its probable (or improbable) facticity.

Within this framework of mastery of content and attention to and respect for the concerns of the biblical writer, there is considerable room for the play of imagination as groups attempt to apply what they have learned to their own situations.

Taking Stock and Moving On

Taking the long view of the problem of biblical authority requires local churches to reexamine their present position *in relation to* a centuries-long relationship between the church and her scriptures. This is true when we wish to convert, or *return*, to a relationship with scripture which seems more authentic because it is rooted in the past. It is perhaps even *more* true when a congregation feels called by God to make a radical departure from a traditional stance—or a change that appears to challenge the authority of scripture in general or on a specific issue. It may be that the change is ultimately in harmony with the biblical mandate; in any case, faithfulness requires that we place ourselves squarely in the midst of this historical relationship as we seek light by which to live.

Finally, it needs to be clarified that a handbook of this nature is not the place to attempt construction of a formal theory of biblical authority. Too often individuals and groups will try to formulate such theories without sufficient practical experience of the Bible's very real (and sometimes awesome) power to change individuals and renew communities. For this reason, a commitment to *take scripture seriously* should take precedence over the popular demand for unequivocal statements about the nature of biblical authority. Listed below are questions designed to help local congregations evaluate the nature of their *actual* (or practical) commitment to scripture and to contrast this with the *formal* claims they make concerning the Bible's authority.

1. What kind of claims do we make for the Bible?
2. What is our response to people who make different claims?
3. Do we use labels to classify or prejudge claims for or responses to scripture?
4. Are we open to dialogue with persons or groups who make different claims for the Bible? Can we provide a suitable context for such discussion?
5. What is the general level of biblical literacy in the community? Does the community take responsibility for the overall level of biblical expertise?
6. How much time does the community allot for the study of scripture? How much in the way of financial resources does the community invest in the study of scripture?
7. How do we *measure* our level of commitment to scripture? By the claims we make, the amount of time and money we invest? the way we pattern our lives?
8. What changes have occurred recently in corporate worship and witness as a consequence of communal dialogue with scripture?

The Difference Study Makes

Do your best to present yourself to God as one approved, a workman who has no need to be ashamed, rightly handling the word of truth.   II Timothy 2:15

The lessons of history may be sobering, but they are also a source of hope for the church today. We are the primary beneficiaries of the church's centuries-long investment in the study of scripture; and we can do something about changing the "unpleasant reality" in which we now find ourselves—a reality characterized by factional strife, mutual distrust, and widespread ignorance.

Our tradition teaches us to expect diversity; it's time we learned also to *respect* it. Our tradition teaches us that creative theologizing is based on a sound and thorough knowledge of the contents of scripture; it's time we made the necessary investment of time and effort to equip ourselves for this task. Our tradition teaches us that the appropriate response to the witness of scripture is conversion and change; it's time for us to acknowledge the Bible's rightful authority in requiring this change of us.

There are many pressures bearing down on the church today—social pressures, time pressures, financial pressures— to say nothing of the terrifying ethical pressures to take stands on complex and controversial questions such as nuclear weapons, economic justice, abortion, and homosexuality. In the face of all this, it may sound unreasonable to issue a call for a substantial increase in the community's commitment of time and energy to a sustained and relatively rigorous study of biblical texts. One may argue that the particular issues with which we must grapple are, for the most part, not directly addressed in scripture and, of course, this is true. However, the issue of who we as the church are and the question of how we are to relate to one another and to the world are directly addressed in scripture, and clarity on *these* issues is essential to faithful decision-making in particular cases.

Furthermore, the very *process* of study has something to teach us beyond the acquisition of content. Practice in exegetical method will do more than help us to understand scripture. It will *re*orient (or "convert") us in relation to the Bible; and, as we work at this task collectively, it will also reorient us in our relationships with one another.

Let us be frank: *exegesis is a discipline.* It teaches us to defer judgment until sufficient data have been collected. It teaches us to treat texts (and, eventually, people) with great care and respect. We learn to listen more attentively to what the text (and our neighbor) has to say before leaping in with a response. We learn to share the responsibilities of research and discussion-leading. We learn to share information first and opinions later. We learn to look at questions contextually, to probe for, collect, sort, and weigh evidence. We learn to measure what we have learned from our faith tradition against the realities of our experience. We learn to subject ourselves to the objective authority of the text before we attempt the mastery of it either as sermon, teaching, or discussion material. Finally, we learn that a direct and immediate relationship with scripture is a source of empowerment and that we are responsible for exercising this power in the reorientation of our lives.

The church's deepest desire and strongest necessity is to anchor itself in a biblical understanding of its identity and mission. Fortunately, the skills and resources needed to achieve this goal are more widely accessible than at any other time in the church's history. Our failure thus far to take advantage of these resources is largely the result of our refusal to recognize that the task of exegesis is a *collective* responsibility— a responsibility that cannot be discharged simply by paying the clergy to do the job for us! Yet even when this collective responsibility has been recognized by congregations, the problem of *how* to initiate and sustain an ongoing and fruitful encounter with the Bible remains; nor has it always been clear that such encounters are the result of *systematic* study and therefore require a substantial commitment of time, energy, and enthusiasm. The guidance and inspiration we seek in scripture are certainly there, but like the treasure hidden in the field or the pearl of great price, their recovery is costly.

Having recognized this, we must also realize that the "price" we are asked to pay is *not* more than we can afford; nor will paying it impoverish us if, along with new skills, we can recover a childlike excitement in discovery and take joy in learning something we never knew before. The goal of *every* discipline is freedom, power, and mastery; and like the athlete who trains countless hours for a single race, the exegete willingly practices a form of submission to the terms of the text for the sake of acquiring a mastery that will express itself in the freedom of fresh insights and with powerful and compelling restatements of ancient truths.

Here we would do well to consider the tradition of study that has been nurtured throughout the centuries by the first "People of the Book," the Jews. This tradition embodies not only a reverent and leisurely (even painstaking) examination of God's *Holy* Word; it also embodies a spirit of playfulness and pleasure in the study of God's *wonder-full* Word. It demonstrates that the hard work of study must be inextricably linked to the discovery of fresh meaning and, consequently, to possibilities for renewal and change. In particular, the prayers of the masters of Hasidic Judaism reflect this ebullient view of study, providing us with a remarkable vision of what it means to reflect on and "enter into" God's Word both with great love and great care. The following, taken from a collection of their work entitled *Your Word Is Fire* is a most suitable prayer for an exegete:

> When you focus all your thought
>   on the power of the words,
>   you may begin to see the sparks of light
>   that shine within them.

CONCLUSIONS

The sacred letters are the chambers
　into which God pours His flowing light.
The lights within each letter, as they touch,
　ignite one another,
　and new lights are born.[1]

It is for these "new lights" and nothing less that we labor.

The Role of Scripture in Our Community

(Congregational Self-study Questionnaire)

1. State briefly your view of the *appropriate* role of scripture in the life of this congregation:

2. How would you characterize the *present* role of scripture in this community?

3. Who or what has contributed most significantly (in either a positive or a negative way) to shaping your view of the Bible and its role in the church? (E.g., a relative, church school teacher, pastor, friend, book, small group, etc.)

4. How would you judge your training in Bible at various periods in your life?

	Good	Fair	Poor	*Denominational Affiliation*
as a child	( )	( )	( )	_____
as a youth	( )	( )	( )	_____
as an adult	( )	( )	( )	_____

5. What are your greatest strengths in the area of Bible study? Your greatest weaknesses?

6. On the average, how much time each day (or each week) do you spend reading or studying scripture?

   How much time do you feel you *should* spend?

   Realistically, how much time *could* you spend?

7. What have been the biggest obstacles to effective and systematic Bible study at church?

   at home?

8. List the Bible study tools you own and check (x) those you use regularly.

9. Rank the following issues from "most troublesome" (#1) to "least troublesome" (#7) *in the context of this congregation.*
   - ( ) Knowledge of biblical content
   - ( ) Differing views of the authority and inspiration of scripture
   - ( ) Opportunities for Bible study
   - ( ) Degree of interest and commitment within congregation
   - ( ) Access to resources
   - ( ) Relevance of scripture to local church programs
   - ( ) Relevance of scripture to current social, political, and ethical issues confronting the church.

10. What consequences, if any, would you anticipate as a result of more exposure to and reflection on the Bible? (Try to be specific.)
   in your personal life:
   in your involvement in church programs:
   in the corporate witness of this community:

11. Do the program committees, boards, and small groups in this community make use of scripture in any way? If so, how?

12. What impact, if any, does the Bible have on program development in this community?

13. How is the Bible used in Sunday worship in this community? What difference would it make if all traces of scripture were removed from the service?

14. What are the things that make this local church a unique community? Do we have a distinctive "mission" to perform? What, if anything, does scripture have to do with shaping our sense of identity and mission?

Glossary

Apocalyptic (Greek: apocalypse = "revelation"): a type of dramatic, visionary, and "sectarian" theology, the most complete examples of which are to be found in the books of Daniel and Revelation. It is characterized by strong, dualistic conceptions of the power of good and evil and belief in a final cataclysmic conflict between these two forces which will bring an end to the world as we know it.

Apocrypha (Greek for "hidden things"): A collection of books found in the *Septuagint*, or Greek translation of the Old Testament, which are not found in the Hebrew Old Testament manuscripts. Roman Catholics, Orthodox, and Protestants differ as to the authority of these books, with Catholics according them the most and Protestants the least.

Biblical criticism: A general term encompassing many methods of studying scripture, all of which rely on the use of reason and standard academic disciplines such as history, linguistics, literature, and sociology. Among the various types of biblical criticism are included:

Form criticism: analysis of the types of literary *genres* or forms found in scripture.

Tradition criticism: analysis of the history of biblical traditions and motifs and the process of their transmission.

Redaction criticism: analysis of the theological perspective of the biblical authors through the study of their writing and editing techniques.

Text criticism: analysis of a biblical text with the intent to recover the original wording.

Canon (transliteration of Greek word which means "to rule"): A collection of books that the church has designated as scriptural or authoritative for faith and practice. Catholic, Protestant, and Orthodox traditions differ as to which books should be considered *canonical.*

Christology (Greek: "knowledge or study of Christ/Anointed One"):

refers to the study of biblical and doctrinal material that sheds light on the person and work of Jesus of Nazareth. In addition to the doctrine of the Incarnation, Christology includes study of the meaning of the titles used for Jesus in the New Testament, e.g., "Son of David," "Son of God," "Son of man," and "Messiah."

Cult (Latin: cultus = "homage" or "devotion"): a system or set of religious practices, including liturgical forms and sacrificial rites. In biblical scholarship it is used to refer to the unique religious rites of ancient Israel. It is not to be confused with bizarre contemporary "cults."

Documentary hypothesis: A by now commonly accepted theory first proposed by Julius Wellhausen, a German theologian of the nineteenth century. Wellhausen postulated four separate authors or sources of the Pentateuch, or the first five books of the Bible, traditionally ascribed to Moses. These sources are designated as follows:
The Jahwist, or "J"
The Elohist, or "E"
The Deuteronomic, or "D"
The Priestly Writer, or "P"

Epiphany (Greek, meaning "manifestation"): sudden appearances of the "divine" in the natural world. Many such incidents are recorded in scripture and are also referred to as *theophanies*, or appearances of God. The incident of the burning bush on Mt. Sinai is referred to as a *theophany*.

Eschatology (from a Greek word meaning "last"): The study of biblical and Christian beliefs about death and resurrection, judgment, heaven, purgatory, and hell. Old Testament passages dealing with the *Day of Yahweh* or the coming of the Messiah or the Son of Man are *eschatalogical* in nature.

Exegesis (Greek for "interpretation"; lit., "guide," or "lead out"): The systematic exposition or interpretation of a text. Methods of exegesis differ, variously reflecting historical, literary, or sociological emphases and perspectives. *Exegetical study* is an attempt to draw meaning out of the text in contrast to *eisegesis*, a derogatory term describing the attempt to read predetermined meanings into a text.

Hermeneutics (Greek for "interpretation" or "translation"): A set of principles and methods for the interpretation of scripture. Both Jesus and Paul employed rabbinic hermeneutical principles in their use of scripture. Hermeneutical theory changes significantly in different historical periods, reflecting the continuous change in intellectual standards and cultural environments.

Kerygma (Greek for "preaching" or "proclamation"): May refer to either the act or content of preaching. A *kerygmatic* passage attempts to elicit a response of faith from the reader.

Oracle (Latin, "oraculum" = a divine message): Scripture contains many "oracles" or utterances from God. These passages occur primarily in the prophetic books. Certain types of *oracular* passages have been identified in the Psalms. *Oracles* are often prefaced with the formula: "Thus saith the Lord . . ."

Oral tradition: A body of traditional material that is carefully memorized and handed on orally to succeeding generations. Much of the material in the *Pentateuch,* the Gospels, and Acts was originally preserved and transmitted in this fashion.

Paraphrase: An attempt to clarify a text through a relatively free rewording—a "translation" of a translation. Paraphrases of the Bible tend to supply additional interpretation as well as additional words, in contrast to translations, which attempt a more or less literal statement of the text. The *Living Bible* is a commonly used paraphrase.

Parousia (Greek for "presence"): Used in scripture and biblical scholarship to refer to the second coming of Christ.

Pentateuch/Torah: Greek and Hebrew terms for the first five books of the Bible, also known as "The Law" or "The Teaching." The term *Hexateuch,* which occurs less frequently, refers to Genesis–Joshua.

Pericope (Greek: "cut around"): a self-contained unit or division of biblical material (a "text") which is isolated for the purpose of study, preaching, or liturgical reading.

Salvation history/Heilsgeschichte (German for "sacred or holy history"): A particular theological perspective or *hermeneutic* espoused by a school of biblical theologians; a recital of the ways in which God has acted on behalf of his chosen people. The central events of salvation history are the Exodus from Egypt and the giving of the Covenant on Mt. Sinai. The Christ-event is seen as a further and culminating event in this history by the New Testament writer Luke.

Septuagint, or LXX (Latin: "seventy"): The first Greek translation of the Hebrew scriptures was, according to tradition, prepared (miraculously) in 70 days by 70 Hebrew scholars! Many of the Old Testament citations contained in the New Testament are based on this version.

Sitz-im-Leben (German for "setting in life"): Bible scholars attempt to "locate" biblical texts in particular social and religious settings in the life of ancient Israel. A particular passage may have been originally used liturgically for a religious festival or as teaching or preaching material, for example.

Synoptics, or Synoptic Gospels (Greek for "with the same eye"): The first three books of the New Testament—Matthew, Mark, and Luke—all of which show striking similarities with one another because of their use of the same sources and possible dependence on one another (in contrast to the Gospel of John).

Wisdom Literature: In contrast to "revelation," Wisdom refers to those books of the Bible (namely, Proverbs, Job, Ecclesiastes, Ecclesiasticus, and the Wisdom of Solomon) which stress humanity's ability to govern itself and to live in right relation with God through reason and "clean living." Scholars are at odds as to how much *Wisdom theology* permeates other parts of the Old Testament, such as the Pentateuch, Psalms, etc.

Yahweh/Elohim/El-Shaddai: Hebrew words used as names for God. Of the three, "Yahweh" is by far the commonest and most significant. Although its actual meaning is unclear, it should be understood as a proper name, not as a title. Spelled with four Hebrew letters YHWH and sometimes referred to as the *Tetragrammaton,* this name is usually rendered as "LORD" out of respect for its sacredness. (The Jerusalem Bible is notable for always translating God's name as Yahweh when it appears that way in the Hebrew text.)

Word Study Instructions

Tools needed: A complete, unabridged concordance such as *Strong's*, *Cruden's*, or *Young's;* a contemporary translation of the English Bible; a copy of the King James Version.

1. Select for study a word that appears central to an understanding of an important theological issue.
   What is your working definition of this word?
   What is the dictionary definition of this word?

2. Scan and analyze the total array of concordance entries for the word, including derivative forms.
   a. *Draw a line between the last O.T. reference and the first N.T. reference.* (Does the word occur significantly more times in one testament than the other?)
   b. *Look for patterns or major groupings of the word within the O.T.* What proportion of the O.T. entries appear in:
      the Law
      the Prophets
      the Writings/History Books
      —the Psalms
      —the Wisdom Literature
      Does a single author/source appear to be the major user of the term in the O.T.?
      Are there places in the O.T. where you would expect to find the word where it is absent or vice versa?
   c. *Look for patterns or major groupings of the word within the N.T. Draw a line between the last entry in Luke–Acts and the first entry in Romans.* (Do the Gospel writers use the word significantly more or less than Paul or other N.T. writers?)
      What proportion of the N.T. entries appear in:
      the Synoptic Gospels (Matthew, Mark, Luke) and Acts
      the Johannine Literature (Gospel of John, I-III John)
      Paul's Letters (Romans–Philemon)
      the Literature of the Early Church (Hebrews, James, I-II Peter, Jude, and Revelation)

Are there places in the N.T. where you would expect to find the word where it is absent or vice versa?

d. *What conclusions do you reach as a result of this preliminary scan of both testaments?* List your conclusions and any further questions you may have at this point in the study.

3. *Examine strategically chosen references, taking note of the larger contexts in which they appear. List those which are most revealing.*

   a. Begin with the testament that has the predominance of references.

   b. O.T. references should include samples from each of the major categories: Law, Prophets, Writings/History Books.

   c. N.T. references should include samples from each of the major categories: Synoptic Gospels and Acts, Johannine Literature, Paul's Letters, The Literature of the Early Church.

   d. *What new information or insights have you gained as a result of the word study? What additional questions has it raised?*

   e. *Are there any logical or conceptual ways of grouping the references other than by author or literary category?*

   f. *Is there any evidence of change, development, or elaboration in the faith community's understanding of this word? At what points do such changes seem to occur?*

4. *Rewrite and/or expand your definition of the word studied.*

5. Reread the biblical passage that led you to do the word study in the first place. How has your research affected your understanding of the passage?

Biblical Exegesis: Step by Step

1. THE INITIAL ANALYSIS (What does the text *say?*)
   a. Before consulting any other resources, read the selected passage in *more than one translation.*
   b. Write a brief *paraphrase* (or restatement) of the passage. Be as concise as possible.

2. CONTENT QUESTIONS (What does the text *mean?*)
   a. *Congregational Context* (Study Selection Principle): *Who* is studying the passage and what is the *purpose* of the study? (Is the passage *one of a series* selected for topical study by a church committee or adult education class? Is the passage the basis for next Sunday's sermon? Is it the next chapter in a biblical book being studied in its entirety?)
   b. *Literary Context:* Read the material immediately preceding and following the selected passage. (This is usually about a chapter's worth of material. If the passage is longer, more surrounding material needs to be read.) How does reading the passage in a larger context affect your interpretation of it? Try to identify the *literary form* of the passage. (Is it a prayer or hymn inserted into narrative material? a collection of wisdom teachings? a prophetic oracle?)
   c. *Canonical Context:* Examine *cross-references* to related and parallel passages mentioned in marginal notes of your study Bible. Use a *concordance* to locate additional related material. Does the author of the biblical passage appear to be relying on earlier biblical traditions? If so, how does the author make use of the earlier material?
   d. *Historical Context:* The historical situation described in the passage is frequently far removed in time from the *historical situation of the author or the audience* to which the passage is addressed. Consult the Bible dictionary entries on the author

and the book in which the passage is contained for information about authorship, dating, and special sources. What *historical or faith crises* confronted Israel/the church at the time this material was most likely written? Does the passage appear to address these crises in any way?

3. VERSE-BY-VERSE ANALYSIS (Does it *mean* what it *says*?)
   a. *Identifying Key Words:* Reread the passage and underline all of the following types of words:
      personal and place names (Noah, Joshua, Jerusalem, Galilee)
      references to important events (the Flood, battle of Jericho)
      references to special objects (brass serpent, Ark of the Covenant)
      references to local customs, religious observances (burial customs, feasts, dietary laws, circumcision, sacrifices)
      any word or phrase that is repeated often, especially verbs ("hear," "I am")
   b. *Use Study Selection Principle* (see 2a above): Select those key words which are most appropriate in view of the study-group's agenda and read selectively from corresponding *Bible dictionary* and *theological wordbook* entries. Take note of information that throws new light on the passage.
   c. *Identifying Theological Themes and Issues:* Most biblical texts address themselves to one or more theological issues/questions. In the process of study these issues become clearer. Sometimes they are easily identified by the author's use of explicit theological language: sin, grace, baptism, messiah, kingdom of God, etc. More often, the issue is presented *indirectly* through the events of a story. As the issues begin to clarify themselves, consult the appropriate entries in the *Bible dictionary* and *theological wordbook* (e.g., articles on "sin" or "sacrifice," etc.) Use the *concordance* to do a *word study* on a key word/theme in the passage.

4. APPLICATIONS *(What difference does it make?)*
   a. *Reread the passage and write a final, "interpretive" paraphrase.* Compare the results with your initial paraphrase. Does the text say what it means? Does it mean more than it appears to say?
   b. *Identify yourself and your congregation in the passage.* With which characters and situations can you most faithfully (i.e., *accurately*) relate? Does the passage sound different "from the inside"? Is its message more painful and compelling?
   c. *What changes does this biblical text at this time require of you and your community?*

1. Beyond the Devotional Bible Study

1. The most notable example of this was Marcion (d. *ca.* A.D. 160), who believed that the God of love revealed in the New Testament had no connection whatsoever with the God of the Law in the Old. He rejected the Old Testament entirely and tried to re-create a truncated version of scripture that contained only the Letters of Paul and an abridged version of Luke. He was excommunicated for his pains in A.D. 144.
2. The consumer/producer image is taken from an unpublished lecture, "The Bible, Christian Education and World Hunger" by Dr. Bruce C. Birch, Professor of Old Testament at Wesley Theological Seminary, Washington, D.C.

2. Equipped to Converse

1. For example, Fortress Press is producing an outstanding series of study books, *Overtures to Biblical Theology,* which are suitable for lay use. A similar series, *Biblical Perspectives on Current Issues,* is being published by Westminster Press. In each case, the focus is topical.
2. Occasionally, one of these gems becomes available to the general public; e.g., Martin Luther's *Commentary on Romans* is available in an attractive paperback format (published by Kregel Publications, Grand Rapids, Michigan 49501, and reprinted in 1979). See also *Calvin: Commentaries,* edited by Joseph Haroutunian (Philadelphia: Westminster Press, no date shown), also available in paperback.
3. A noteworthy example of this is the *Genesis to Revelation* series published by Graded Press, the curriculum publishing department of The United Methodist Publishing House. This series, currently in the making, seeks to do justice to biblical texts by first focusing on what the texts *say* before attempting to state what the texts mean.

3. Places to Talk

1. For example, see the following *series: Proclamation Commentaries* and *Proclamation Aids for Interpreting the Church Year* (Fortress Press); *Knox Preaching Guides* (John Knox); *The Liturgical Year* (The Liturgical Press); *The Sunday Readings* (Franciscan Herald Press); *This Is the Word of the Lord* (Oxford University Press); and *Guide for the Christian Assembly* (Fides/Claretian Press).
2. In designing and testing a lectionary study method, I was delighted to find that one of the chief outcomes of lectionary study for the laity is a greatly enhanced appreciation for the Old Testament and a much clearer understanding of how Old Testament traditions are important for understanding the New Testament.

4. Learning the Language

1. E. C. Blackman, "Know, Knowledge," in *A Theological Wordbook of the Bible,* ed. Alan Richardson (New York: Macmillan, 1950), pp. 121-22.
2. L. H. Brockington, "Hear, Hearken, Ear, Listen," in *ibid.,* p. 104.
3. Alan Richardson, "Abraham," in *ibid.,* pp. 12-13.

4. "Abraham," in *The New Harper's Bible Dictionary*, ed. Madeleine S. and J. Lane Miller (New York: Harper & Row, 1973), pp. 3-4.

5. Quoted in Donald G. Millar, "Concordances," in *Tools for Bible Study*, ed. Balmer Kelly and Donald G. Miller (Richmond: John Knox Press, 1956), p. 10.

6. Harold K. Moulton, *The Challenge of the Concordance: Some New Testament Words Studied in Depth* (Greenwood, S.C.: The Attic Press, 1977), p. xiii.

7. Although it is true that "redeem" is not used by other Gospel writers, the closely related word "ransom" appears in a saying of Jesus recorded in Matthew 20:28 and Mark 10:45: "The Son of man also came not to be served but to serve, and to give his life a ransom for many." It is unfortunate that *Strong's* does not cross-reference the student to "ransom" since its connection to "redeem" is so obvious. The absolute numbers and percentages shown in this word study reflect the biblical writers' use of the Greek and Hebrew words for "redeem/redemption" only and do not include references to "ransom." Were they to be included they would not significantly alter the results of the word study except perhaps to increase slightly the proportion of entries from the wisdom literature. The most significant omission is the saying of Jesus mentioned above.

8. Quoted from the unsigned preface of the *New International Version* (New York: The New York International Bible Society, 1978), p. vii.

9. Roman Catholic Bibles contain the following Deuterocanonical books in addition to the books contained in the Protestant canon: Tobit, Judith, additions to Esther, I-II Maccabees, the Book of Wisdom, Ecclesiasticus (or Sirach), Baruch, and additions to Daniel.

10. Alexander Jones, "Editor's Foreword to the Reader's Edition," *Jerusalem Bible Reader's Edition* (Garden City, N.Y.: Doubleday, 1968), p. v.

11. Prior to 1943 all Roman Catholic translations of scripture were based on the Latin Vulgate Bible.

12. This and other quotes from Kenneth Taylor are from his preface to *The Living Bible Paraphrased New Testament* (Wheaton, Ill.: Tyndale House Publishers, 1971), p. xv.

13. For an excellent survey of the most popular English versions of the Bible see Robert G. Bratcher, "One Bible in Many Translations," in *Interpretation* XXXII (April, 1978), 115-29.

14. J. B. Phillips, "Introduction" to *The New Testament in Modern English*, rev. ed. (New York: Macmillan, 1972), p. xxix.

15. Some might wish to quarrel with my classification of particular versions as either "dynamic equivalents" or "closest equivalent possible." A certain amount of subjectivity in judgments such as these is inevitable.

6. The Bible Has the First Word

1. Commentaries are often extremely helpful but somewhat seductive to the beginning student. The authoritative manner in which the commentator's interpretation of the passage is presented tends to discourage an imaginative (or different) response from the student, who naturally feels hesitant about disagreeing with an "authority" who has made it into print! In the end, the habit of relying on commentaries may become a *substitute* for serious individual study.

7. The Community Responds

1. The material in this section relating to basic and follow-up questions is essentially a re-application of a questioning technique used in the Great

Books training programs. The Great Books training manuals (Great Books Foundation, Chicago) provide numerous examples of this and other discussion techniques that may be used in a variety of settings whenever and wherever one's goal is to foster more critical, reflective thinking.

2. It must be admitted, however, that much of this type of information is truly fascinating in its own right. It should never be dismissed as "irrelevant," especially when presented by an enthusiastic participant who was either amazed, delighted, or horrified by what he found.

8. The Spirit Has the Last Word

1. Krister Stendahl, *Paul Among Jews and Gentiles* (Philadelphia: Fortress Press), 1976, p. 38.
2. For example, Joachim Jeremias, *Rediscovering the Parables* (New York: Charles Scribner's Sons), 1966; see especially pages 111ff. Few Bible scholars do a better job than Professor Jeremias in supplying the kind of background information that is essential to understanding the world view of the New Testament.
3. Herbert Bronstein, ed., *A Passover Haggadah*, rev. ed. (New York: Central Conference of American Rabbis, 1974, 1975), p. 53.
4. Brevard S. Childs, *Memory and Tradition in Israel* (Naperville, Ill.: Alec R. Allenson), 1967, pp. 83-84.

9. First and Last Words

1. See *Peter in the New Testament: A Collaborative Assessment by Protestant and Roman Catholic Scholars,* ed. Raymond E. Brown, Karl P. Donfried, and John Reumann (Minneapolis: Augsburg Press; and New York: Paulist Press, 1973). This work was sponsored by the United States Lutheran–Roman Catholic Dialogue as Background for Ecumenical Discussions of the Role of the Papacy in the Universal Church. See also, *Mary in the New Testament: A Collaborative Assessment by Protestant and Roman Catholic Scholars,* ed. Raymond E. Brown, Karl P. Donfried, Joseph A. Fitzmyer, and John Reumann (Philadelphia: Fortress Press; and New York: Paulist Press, 1978). This work was also sponsored by the United States Lutheran–Roman Catholic Dialogue.
2. Eusebius, *Ecclesiastical History,* 6, 2, 1, quoted in Jean Danielou, *Origen,* translated by Walter Mitchell (New York: Sheed and Ward, 1955), pp. 4-5.
3. All quotations from Origen are taken from his "Commentary on John," *Ante-Nicene Christian Library,* vol. IX, X16, ed. Allan Menzies (Edinburgh: T. & T. Clark, 1897).
4. Saint Augustine, *Confessions,* Book V. 14, translated and with an introduction by R. S. Pine-Coffin (Harmondsworth, Middlesex, England: Penguin Books, 1961), p. 108.

Conclusions

1. Reprinted from *Your Word Is Fire* by Arthur Green and Barry W. Holtz. © 1977 by Arthur Green and Barry W. Holtz. Used by permission of Paulist Press.

BIBLIOGRAPHY

Biblical Preaching (Chapter 3)

Buechner, Frederick. *Telling the Truth: The Gospel as Tragedy, Comedy, and Fairy Tale*. New York: Harper & Row, 1977.
Duke, Robert W. *The Sermon as God's Word: Theologies for Preaching*. Nashville: Abingdon, 1980.
Fuller, Reginald. *Preaching the New Lectionary*. Collegeville, Minn.: The Liturgical Press, 1974.
Gowan, Donald. *Reclaiming the Old Testament for the Christian Pulpit*. Atlanta: John Knox, 1981.
Keck, Leander. *The Bible in the Pulpit*. Nashville: Abingdon, 1978.
Knox, John. *The Integrity of Preaching*. Nashville: Abingdon Press, 1957.
Rad, Gerhard von. *Biblical Interpretations in Preaching*, trans. John E. Steely. Nashville: Abingdon, 1977.
Skudlarek, William. *The Word in Worship: Preaching in a Liturgical Context*. Nashville: Abingdon, 1981.
Steimle, Edmund A. *Preaching the Story*. Philadelphia: Fortress, 1980.
Stookey, Lawrence. *Living in a New Age*. Lima, Ohio: C.S.S. Publishing Co., 1978.

Learning the Language (Chapter 4)

Technical Terms

Cully, Iris V., and Cully, Kendig Brubaker. *An Introductory Theological Wordbook*. Philadelphia: Westminster Press, 1963.
Harvey, Van A. *A Handbook of Theological Terms*. New York: Macmillan, 1964.
Soulen, Richard N. *Handbook of Biblical Criticism*. Atlanta: John Knox Press, 1976.
Warshaw, Thayer S. *Abingdon Glossary of Religious Terms*. Nashville: Abingdon, 1980.

Resources for Developing a Biblical Vocabulary

Allmen, J.-J. von. *A Companion to the Bible*. New York: Oxford University Press, 1951.
Bauer, J. B., ed. *Encyclopedia of Biblical Theology: The Complete Sacramentum Verbi*. New York: Crossroads Publishing Co., 1981.
Leon-Dufour, Xavier. *Dictionary of Biblical Theology*, 2nd ed. (New York: Seabury Press, 1973.
————. *Dictionary of the New Testament*. New York: Harper & Row, 1980.
Neill, Stephen; Goodwin, John; and Doule, Arthur, eds. *The Modern Reader's Dictionary of the Bible*. New York: Association Press, 1966.

Richardson, Alan, ed. *A Theological Wordbook of the Bible.* New York: Macmillan, 1950.

Vine, W. E. *An Expository Dictionary of New Testament Words.* Nashville: Thomas Nelson, 1978.

————. *An Expository Dictionary of Old Testament Words.* Old Tappan, N.J.: Revell, 1978.

Multi-Volume Bible Dictionaries Suitable for Church Libraries

Bromily, Geoffrey W., ed. *International Standard Bible Encyclopedia,* rev. Grand Rapids: W. B. Eerdmans, vol. I, 1979; vol. II, 1981.

Buttrick, George A., and Crim, Keith R., eds. *The Interpreter's Dictionary of the Bible: An Illustrated Encyclopedia,* 5 vols. Nashville: Abingdon Press, 1963 and 1976.

Tenney, Merrill C., ed. *The New Zondervan Pictorial Encyclopedia,* 5 vols. Grand Rapids: Zondervan, 1974.

One-Volume Bible Dictionaries Reflecting the Views of Conservative Scholarship

Douglass, J. D., ed. *The New Bible Dictionary.* Grand Rapids: W. B. Eerdmans, 1962.

Tenney, Merrill C., ed. *Zondervan Pictorial Bible Dictionary.* Grand Rapids: Zondervan, 1969.

Unger, Merrill F., ed. *Unger's Bible Dictionary.* Evanston, Ill.: Moody Press, 1961.

One-Volume Bible Dictionaries Reflecting the Views of Historical-Critical Scholarship

Gehman, Henry S., ed. *The New Westminster Dictionary of the Bible.* Philadelphia: Westminster Press, 1970.

McKenzie, John L., S.J. *Dictionary of the Bible.* New York: Macmillan, 1965.

Miller, Madeleine S., and Lane, J., eds. *The New Harper's Bible Dictionary.* New York: Harper & Row, 1973.

Concordances

Cruden, Alexander. *Concordance to the Old and New Testaments* (1737). Editions by several publishers; available in hard and soft covers. Make sure the edition used is complete and not abridged. Based on the King James Version.

Ellison, John William. *Nelson's Complete Concordance of the Revised Standard Version of the Bible.* Camden, N.J.: Thomas Nelson & Sons, 1957.

Hartdegen, Stephen J., ed. *Nelson's Complete Concordance of the New American Bible.* Nashville: Thomas Nelson, 1977.

Hazard, Marshall Custiss. *A Complete Concordance to the American Standard Version of the Holy Bible.* London: Thomas Nelson & Sons, 1922.

Joy, Charles R., ed. *Harper's Topical Concordance*, rev. and enlarged ed. New York: Harper and Bros., 1962.

Miller, D. M., ed. *The Topical Bible Concordance*. Nashville: Abingdon, 1977.

Morrison, Clinton. *Analytical Concordance to the Revised Standard Version of the New Testament*. Philadelphia: Westminster Press, 1979.

Strong, James. *Strong's Exhaustive Concordance*. Editions by several publishers; available in hard and soft covers. Based on the King James Version.

Thompson, Newton Wayland, and Stock, Raymond. *Complete Concordance to the Bible* (Douay-Rheims Version). St. Louis: B. Herder Book Co., 1945.

Young, Robert. *Analytical Concordance to the Bible, revised*. Grand Rapids: W. B. Eerdmans, 1955. Based on the King James Version.

For more help in learning how to use a concordance, consult:

Miller, Donald G. "Concordances," in *Tools for Bible Study*, ed. Balmer Kelly and Donald G. Miller. Richmond: John Knox Press, 1956.

Moulton, Harold K. *The Challenge of the Concordance: Some New Testament Words Studied in Depth*. Greenwood, S.C.: Attic Press, 1977.

Additional Reading on the History of the English Bible

Beegle, Dewey. *God's Word into English*. New York: Harper and Bros., 1960.

Bowne, Dale Russell. *How to Choose a Bible*. Livermore, Cal.: Griggs Educational Service, 1979. Excellent, but currently out of print.

Bratcher, Robert G. "One Bible in Many Translations," in *Interpretation*, vol. 2, no. 2 (April, 1978), pp. 115-29.

Bratcher, Robert G. *Why So Many Bibles?* New York: American Bible Society, 1968.

Bruce, F. F. *History of the Bible in English*, 3rd edition. New York: Oxford University Press, 1978.

Cully, Iris V., and Cully, Kendig Brubaker. *A Guide to Biblical Resources*. Wilton, Conn.: Morehouse-Barlow Co., 1981. See pp. 1-55.

Goodspeed, Edgar. *How Came the Bible?* Nashville: Abingdon Festival Book, 1976.

Hutchison, Warner, "Selecting a Bible: Which Translation?" in *Living Light*, vol. 17, no. 4 (Winter, 1980), pp. 350-56.

Kubo, Sakae, and Specht, Walter. *So Many Versions?* Grand Rapids: Zondervan, 1975.

MacGregor, Geddes. *The Bible in the Making*. Philadelphia: Lippincott, 1959.

———. *A Literary History of the Bible from the Middle Ages to the Present Day*. Nashville: Abingdon Press, 1968.

May, Herbert Gordon. *Our English Bible in the Making: The Word of Life in Living Language*. Philadelphia: Westminster Press, 1965.

Nida, Eugene A. *God's Word in Man's Language*. New York: Harper and Bros., 1952.

———— and William, Reyburn. *Meaning Across Cultures*. Maryknoll, N.Y.: Orbis Books, 1981.

Recommended Study Bibles

The New Oxford Annotated Bible with the Apocrypha, expanded edition. New York: Oxford University Press, 1977. Available without Apocrypha.

The New English Bible with the Apocrypha, Oxford Study Edition. New York: Oxford University Press, 1976. Available without the Apocrypha.

The Jerusalem Bible. Garden City, N.Y.: Doubleday, 1966.

The New American Bible, Saint Joseph's Edition. Catholic Book Publishing Co., 1970.

The Good News Bible with Deuterocanonicals/Apocrypha. New York: American Bible Society, 1979.

American Standard Version, Standard Edition. Thomas Nelson Publishers, 1901.

New American Standard Version, Reference Edition. New York: Collins-World, 1973.

New International Version, Standard Edition. Grand Rapids: Zondervan Bible Publishers, 1978. Not really a full-scale "study Bible." Maps are the only extra feature. Format is excellent.

Supplementary Bibles Available in Softcover Editions

Jerusalem Bible, Reader's Edition. Garden City, N.Y.: Doubleday, 1968.

New American Bible. Nashville: Thomas Nelson, 1980.

King James Bible. Cleveland: World Publishing Company.

The New English Bible with Apocrypha. New York: Oxford University Press, 1972.

The Good News Bible with Deuterocanonicals/Apocrypha. New York: American Bible Society, 1979.

J. B. Phillips. *The New Testament in Modern English*, revised edition. New York: Macmillan, 1972.

The Common Bible: Revised Standard Version. Nashville: Thomas Nelson, 1973.

Multi-Version Bibles

The Eight-Translation New Testament. Wheaton, Ill.: Tyndale House Publishers, 1974.

The Layman's Parallel Bible. Grand Rapids: Zondervan, 1973.

The Layman's Parallel New Testament. Grand Rapids: Zondervan, 1970.

Parallels and Synopses

Aland, Kurt, ed. *Synopsis of the Four Gospels*, Greek-English edition of the *Synopsis Quattuor Evangeliorum* with the Text of the *Revised Standard Version*, 3rd ed. United Bible Societies, 1979.

Burton, Ernest DeWitt, and Goodspeed, Edgar Johnson. *A Harmony of the Synoptic Gospels: For Historical and Critical Study.* New York: Charles Scribner's Sons, 1929.

Flanagan, Neal M., O.S.M. *Mark, Matthew, Luke: A Guide to the Gospel Parallels.* Collegeville, Minn.: The Liturgical Press, 1978. A companion to Throckmorton's *Gospel Parallels.*

Francis, Fred O., and Sampley, J. Paul. *Pauline Parallels.* Philadelphia: Fortress Press, 1975.

Sparks, H. F. D. *The Johannine Synopsis of the Gospels.* New York: Harper & Row, 1974.

Throckmorton, Burton H., Jr., ed. *Gospel Parallels.* New York: Thomas Nelson, 1967.

One-Volume Commentaries

Black, Matthew, and Rowley, H. H., eds. *Peake's Commentary on the Bible,* completely revised ed. New York: Nelson, 1962.

Brown, Raymond, *et al.,* eds. *The Jerome Biblical Commentary.* Englewood Cliffs, N.J.: Prentice-Hall, 1969.

Eiselen, Frederick Carl, *et al.,* eds. *The Abingdon Bible Commentary.* Published in hardcover edition by Abingdon Press, 1929, and in a softcover edition by Doubleday & Co., 1979.

Howley, G. C. D., *et al.,* eds. *The New Layman's Bible Commentary.* Zondervan, 1979.

Laymon, Charles M. *The Interpreter's One-Volume Commentary on the Bible.* Nashville: Abingdon Press, 1971.

Neil, William, *Harper's Bible Commentary.* New York: Harper & Row, 1962.

Individual Bible Commentary Series

Anchor Bible Series. Garden City, N.Y.: Doubleday.

Cambridge Bible Commentary Series. Cambridge: Cambridge University Press.

Daily Bible Study Series. Philadelphia: Westminster Press.

Harper's New Testament Commentaries. New York: Harper & Row.

Image Books Commentaries ("Invitation" Series). Garden City, N.Y.: Doubleday.

Interpretation Commentaries. Atlanta: John Knox Press.

New Century Bible Commentaries. Grand Rapids: W. B. Eerdmans.

New International Commentaries. Grand Rapids: W. B. Eerdmans.

Old and New Testament Reading Guide Series. Collegeville, Minn.: The Liturgical Press.

Old Testament Library. Philadelphia: Westminster Press.

Pelican New Testament Commentaries. Penguin Books. Also published as the Westminster Pelican Commentaries. Philadelphia: Westminster Press.

Proclamation Commentaries. Philadelphia: Fortress Press.

Bible Atlases

Aharoni, Yohanon, and Avi-Yonah, Michael, eds. *The Macmillan Bible Atlas,* revised edition. New York: Macmillan, 1977.

Frank, Harry T., ed. *Hammond's Atlas of the Bible Lands.* Maplewood, N.J.: Hammond, 1977.

Grollenberg, Luc H. *The Penguin Shorter Atlas of the Bible,* Mary F. Hedlund, trans. New York: Penguin Books, 1978.

May, Herbert G. *Oxford Bible Atlas,* 2nd ed. New York: Oxford University Press, 1974.

Monson, J. Student. *Map Manual: Historical Geography of the Holy Land.* Published by Pictorial Archive: Near Eastern History in Jerusalem, and distributed by Zondervan, 1979.

Pfeiffer, Charles F., and Vos, Howard F. *The Wycliffe Historical Geography of Bible Lands.* Evanston, Ill.: Moody Press, 1967.

Wright, G. Ernest, and Wilson, Floyd V., eds. *Westminster Historical Maps of Bible Lands.* Philadelphia: Westminster Press, 1952.

The Sacred Land. Overlays prepared by the editors of the *World Book Year Book.* Nashville: A. J. Holman Co., 1966.

Sources of Additional Bibliography

Childs, Brevard S. *Old Testament Books for Pastor and Teacher.* Philadelphia: Westminster, 1977.

Cully, Iris V., and Cully, Kendig Brubaker. *A Guide to Biblical Resources.* Wilton, Conn.: Morehouse-Barlow Co., 1981.

Supplemental Resources

Study of Biblical Books

Anderson, Bernhard. *Out of the Depths: The Psalms Speak for Us Today.* Philadelphia: Westminster Press, 1974.

Birch, Bruce C. *Singing the Lord's Song: A Study of Isaiah 40–55.* Prepared by the Education and Cultivation Division for the Women's Division, General Board of Global Ministries, The United Methodist Church, 1981.

Bottoms, Laurence. *Ecclesiastes Speaks to Us Today.* Atlanta: John Knox Press, 1979.

Cannon, William R. *Jesus the Servant: From the Gospel of Mark.* Nashville: The Upper Room, 1978.

Cassidy, Richard J. *Jesus, Politics, and Society: A Study of Luke's Gospel.* Maryknoll, N.Y.: Orbis Books, 1978.

Croatto, J. Severino. *Exodus: A Hermeneutics of Freedom.* Maryknoll, N.Y.: Orbis Books, 1981.

Edwards, O. C. *Luke's Story of Jesus.* Philadelphia: Fortress Press, 1981.

Effird, James M. *Jeremiah: Prophet Under Siege.* Valley Forge, Pa.: Judson Press, 1979.

Eller, Vernard. *The Most Revealing Book in the Bible: Making Sense Out of Revelation.* Grand Rapids: W. B. Eerdmans, 1974.

Ellul, Jacque. *The Judgment of Jonah.* Grand Rapids: W. B. Eerdmans, 1971.

———. *The Politics of God and the Politics of Man.* Grand Rapids: W. B. Eerdmans, 1972. (On II Kings.)

Ewing, Ward B. *Job: A Vision of God.* New York: Seabury Press Crossroad Book, 1976.

Fretheim, Terence. *The Message of Jonah.* Minneapolis: Augsburg Publishing House, 1977.

Hamlin, John E. *Comfort My People: A Guide to Isaiah 40–66.* Atlanta: John Knox Press, 1979.

Holladay, William L. *Isaiah: Scroll of a Prophetic Heritage.* Grand Rapids: W. B. Eerdmans, 1978.

Kysar, Robert. *John the Maverick Gospel.* Atlanta: John Knox Press, 1976.

Napier, Davie. *Word of God, Word of Earth.* Philadelphia: United Church Press, 1976. (On I Kings.)

Scammon, John. *If I Could Find God: Anguish and Faith in the Book of Job.* Valley Forge, Pa.: Judson Press, 1974.

Tannehill, Robert C. *A Mirror for Disciples: A Study of the Gospel of Mark.* Nashville: Discipleship Resources, 1977.

Walters, Carl, Jr. *I, Mark: A Personal Encounter.* Atlanta: John Knox Press, 1980.

White, R. E. O. *The Mind of Matthew.* Philadelphia: Westminster Press, 1977.

> *N.B.* In addition to the single titles listed above, some series designed to accompany the lectionary are suitable supplementary resources for the study of a single book, e.g., *Proclamation Commentaries* (published by Fortress Press) are not really "commentaries" in the conventional sense but interpretive essays. *The Knox Preaching Guides* and a new series planned by Augsburg Publishing House also fall into this category.

Survey Studies of the Bible

Achtemeier, Paul J. and Elizabeth. *The Old Testament Roots of Our Faith.* Philadelphia: Fortress Press, 1962.

Anderson, Bernhard W. *The Unfolding Drama of the Bible.* Piscataway, N.Y.: Association Press, New Century Publishers, 1971.

Davies, W. D. *Invitation to the New Testament: A Guide to Its Main Witnesses.* Garden City, N.Y.: Doubleday Anchor Books, 1969.

de Dietrich, Suzanne. *God's Unfolding Purpose.* Philadelphia: Westminster Press, 1976.

———. *The Witnessing Community: The Biblical Record.* Philadelphia: Westminster Press, 1958.

Effird, James M. *These Things Are Written: An Introduction to the Religious Ideas of the Bible.* Atlanta: John Knox Press, 1978.

Keck, Leander E. *The New Testament Experience of Faith.* St. Louis: Bethany Press, 1976.

Napier, Davie. *Song of the Vineyard: A Guide Through the Old Testament.* Philadelphia: Fortress Press, 1962.

Neill, Stephen. *Jesus Through Many Eyes: Introduction to the Theology of the New Testament.* Philadelphia: Fortress Press, 1976.

Rendtorff, Rolf. *God's History: A Way Through the Old Testament.* Philadelphia: Westminster Press, 1969.

Sandmel, Samuel. *The Hebrew Scriptures.* New York: Oxford University Press, 1978.

Shannon, David. *The Old Testament Experience of Faith.* Valley Forge, Pa.: Judson Press, 1977.

Wright, G. Ernest, and Fuller, Reginald H. *The Book of the Acts of God: Contemporary Scholarship Interprets the Bible.* Garden City, N.Y.: Doubleday Anchor Books, 1960.

Interpreting Biblical Texts is a new series by Abingdon which nicely complements survey studies. Titles include:

Bailey, Lloyd R. *The Pentateuch,* 1981.

Fretheim, Terence. *The Deuteronomic History,* 1983 (projected).

Ward, James. *The Prophets,* 1982.

Murphy, Roland. *The Wisdom Literature,* 1983.

Hanson, Paul. *Old Testament Apocalyptic,* 1984 (projected).

Craddock, Fred B. *The Gospels,* 1981.

Furnish, Victor, and Keck, Leander. *The Pauline Letters,* 1984 (projected).

Minear, Paul S. *New Testament Apocalyptic Literature,* 1981.

Topical Bible Study

Aukerman, Dale. *The Darkening Valley: A Biblical Perspective on Nuclear War.* New York: Seabury Press, 1981.

Brueggemann, Walter. *Living Toward a Vision: Biblical Reflections on Shalom.* Philadelphia: United Church Press, 1976.

———. *The Prophetic Imagination.* Philadelphia: Fortress Press, 1978.

Daly, Robert J. *The Origins of the Christian Doctrine of Sacrifice.* Philadelphia: Westminster Press, 1978.

Eller, Vernard. *War and Peace: From Genesis to Revelation.* Scottsdale, Pa.: Herald Press, 1981.

Furnish, Victor Paul. *The Moral Teaching of Paul: Selected Issues.* Nashville: Abingdon, 1979.

Hillers, Delbert R. *Covenant: The History of a Biblical Idea.* Baltimore: Johns Hopkins Press, 1969.

Minear, Paul S. *Images of the Church in the New Testament.* Philadelphia: Westminster Press, 1960.

Otwell, John H. *And Sarah Laughed: The Status of Women in the Old Testament.* Philadelphia: Westminster Press, 1977.

Pilgrim, Walter E. *Good News to the Poor: Wealth and Poverty in Luke-Acts.* Minneapolis: Augsburg Publishing House, 1981.

Pixley, George V. *God's Kingdom.* Maryknoll, N.Y.: Orbis Books, 1981.

Sider, Ronald J. *Rich Christians in an Age of Hunger: A Biblical Study.* Downers Grove, Ill.: Intervarsity Press, 1977.

Simundson, Daniel J. *Faith Under Fire: Biblical Interpretations of Suffering.* Minneapolis: Augsburg Publishing House, 1980.

Westermann, Claus. *God's Angels Need No Wings.* Philadelphia: Fortress Press, 1979.

The following series make excellent resources for topical study:

I.   Biblical Encounters Series (Abingdon)
   Eckart, Otto, and Schramm, Tim. *Festival and Joy,* 1980.
   Gerstenberger, E. S., and Schrage, W. *Suffering,* 1977.
   Günneweg, Antonius H. J., and Schmithals, Walter. *Achievement,* 1981.
   Hermann, Siegfried. *Time and History,* 1981.
   Hermisson, Hans Jürgen, and Lohse, Eduard. *Faith,* 1981.
   Kaiser, Otto, and Lohse, Eduard. *Death and Life,* 1981.
   Steck, Odil Hannes. *World and Environment,* 1980.

II. Overtures to Biblical Theology Series (Fortress Press)
   Bailey, Lloyd R., Sr. *Biblical Perspectives on Death,* 1979.
   Brueggemann, Walter. *The Land: Place as Gift, Promise, and Challenge,* 1977.
   Hamerton-Kelly, Robert. *God the Father: Theology and Patriarchy in the Teaching of Jesus,* 1979.
   Hanson, Paul D. *The Diversity of Scripture: Trajectories in the Confessional Heritage,* 1982.
   Harrelson, Walter. *The Ten Commandments and Human Rights,* 1980.
   Harrington, Daniel J., S.J. *God's People in Christ: New Testament Perspectives on the Church and Judaism,* 1980.
   Johnson, Luke T. *Sharing Possessions: Mandate and Symbol of Faith,* 1981.
   Klein, Ralph W. *Israel in Exile: A Theological Interpretation,* 1979.
   Patrick, Dale. *The Rendering of God in the Old Testament,* 1981.
   Trible, Phyllis. *God and the Rhetoric of Sexuality,* 1978.
   Westermann, Claus. *Blessing in the Bible and the Life of the Church,* 1978.

III. Biblical Perspectives on Current Issues Series (Westminster Press)
   Achtemeier, Elizabeth. *The Committed Marriage,* 1976.
   Achtemeier, Paul J. *The Inspiration of Scripture,* 1980.
   Birch, Bruce C., and Rasmussen, Larry L. *The Predicament of the Prosperous,* 1978.
   Shriver, Donald W. and Ostrom, Karl A. *Is There Hope for the City?* 1977.
   Sloyan, Gerard S. *Is Christ the End of the Law?* 1978.

Swearer, Donald K. *Dialogue: The Key to Understanding Other Religions,* 1977.
Towner, W. Sibley. *How God Deals with Evil,* 1976.

For Leaders of Topical Bible Studies

Birch, Bruce C., and Rasmussen, Larry L. *The Bible and Ethics in the Christian Life.* Minneapolis: Augsburg Publishing House, 1976.
Everding, H. Edward, and Wilbanks, Dana W. *Decision-Making and the Bible.* Valley Forge, Pa.: Judson Press, 1975.

9. First and Last Words

Achtemeier, Paul J. *The Inspiration of Scripture: Problems and Prospects.* Philadelphia: Westminster Press, 1980.
Beegle, Dewey M. *Scripture, Tradition, and Infallibility.* Grand Rapids: William B. Eerdmans, 1973.
Grant, Robert M. *A Short History of the Interpretation of the Bible.* New York: Macmillan, 1963.
Rogers, Jack B., and McKim, Donald K. *The Authority and Interpretation of the Bible: An Historical Approach.* New York: Harper & Row, 1979.
Smart, James. *The Interpretation of Scripture.* London: SCM Press, 1961.
Vawter, Bruce. *Theological Resources: Biblical Inspiration.* Philadelphia: Westminster Press, 1972.